Reminiscences of Conrad S. Babcock

The American Military Experience Series
John C. McManus, Series Editor

The books in this series portray and analyze the experience of Americans in military service during war and peacetime from the onset of the twentieth century to the present. The series emphasizes the profound impact wars have had on nearly every aspect of recent American history and considers the significant effects of modern conflict on combatants and noncombatants alike. Titles in the series include accounts of battles, campaigns, and wars; unit histories; biographical and autobiographical narratives; investigations of technology and warfare; studies of the social and economic consequences of war; and in general, the best recent scholarship on Americans in the modern armed forces. The books in the series are written and designed for a diverse audience that encompasses nonspecialists as well as expert readers.

Reminiscences of Conrad S. Babcock

The Old U.S. Army and the New 1898–1918

EDITED BY
Robert H. Ferrell

University of Missouri Press Columbia and London

University of Missouri Press, Columbia, Missouri 65201
Printed and bound in the United States of America

5 4 3 2 1 16 15 14 13 12

Cataloging-in-Publication data available from the Library of Congress.
ISBN 978-0-8262-1981-7

♾™ This paper meets the requirements of the
American National Standard for Permanence of Paper
for Printed Library Materials, Z39.48, 1984.

Designer: Kristie Lee
Typesetter: K. Lee Design & Graphics
Printer and binder: Integrated Book Technology
Typefaces: Palatino

Contents

Acknowledgments

All maps are from *American Armies and Battlefields in Europe*, the army's official guide published under the supervision of General John J. Pershing: it was reprinted by the army's Center of Military History in 1995. Several maps contain signs for stops and arrows for routes, referring readers to portions of the guide's text.

My thanks to two research librarians at Indiana University, Jeffrey C. Graf and Louise Malcomb, and to three friends for advice along the way—Edward M. Coffman, John S. D. Eisenhower, and Beverly Jarrett. Readers for the University of Missouri Press were most helpful: Carlo d'Este and John C. McManus. I am grateful indeed for inclusion in the latter's American Military Experience Series. Richard J. Sommers of the U.S. Army Military History Institute, a part of the Army War College at Carlisle Barracks, Carlisle, Pennsylvania, extended the hospitality of his extraordinary library and manuscript collection. Similarly at the National Archives in College Park, Maryland, I am indebted to Timothy Nenninger and Mitchell A. Yockelson. At the University of Missouri Press my thanks to Dwight Browne, director; Clair Willcox, editor-in-chief; Sara Davis, managing editor; and Kristie Lee, designer. Betty Bradbury did the word processing. My appreciation to the index alphabetizers Carolyn and Lorin and to their assistants Amanda and Samantha.

Diagrammatic Sketch of Western Front Showing Certain Topographical Features of Military Importance

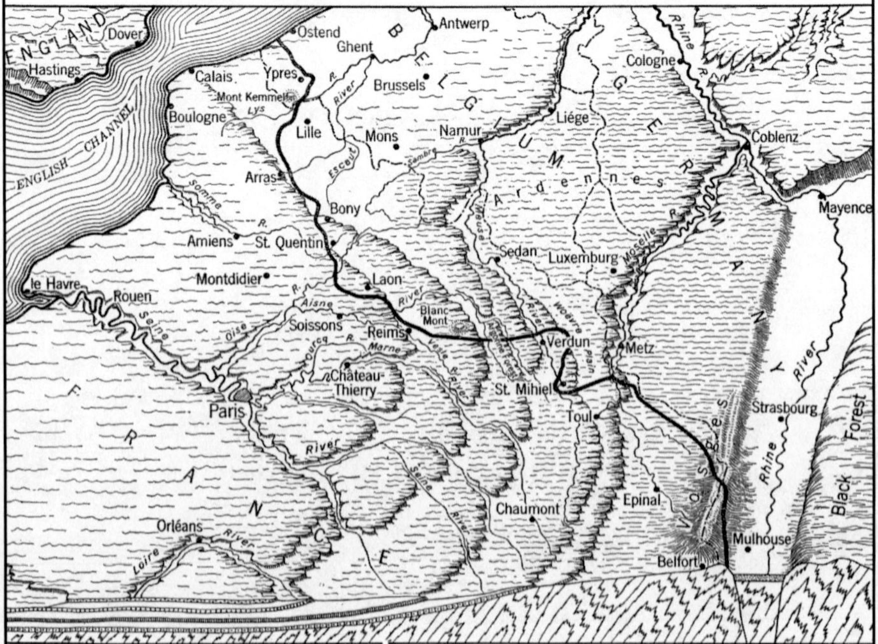

Front Line of March 20, 1918 — International Boundary

Ground Gained by German Offensives of May, June and July, 1918

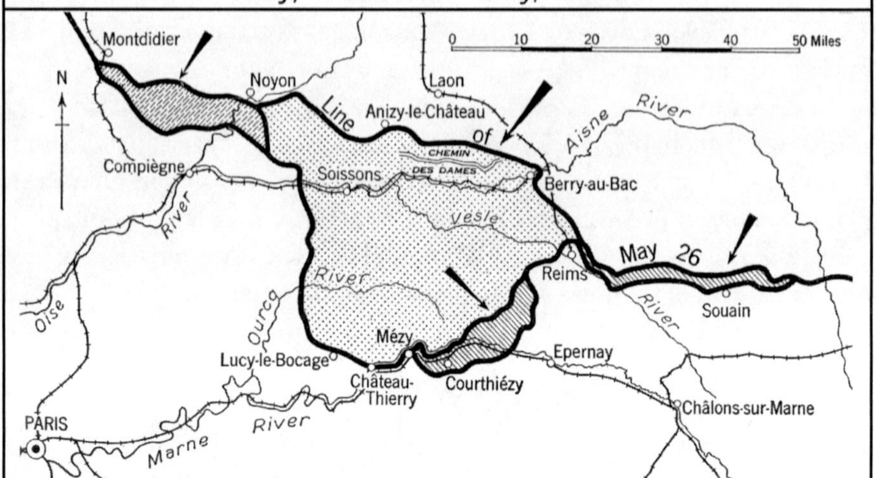

May 27-June 5 | June 9-13 | July 15-17

French-American Counteroffensive, July 18, 1918

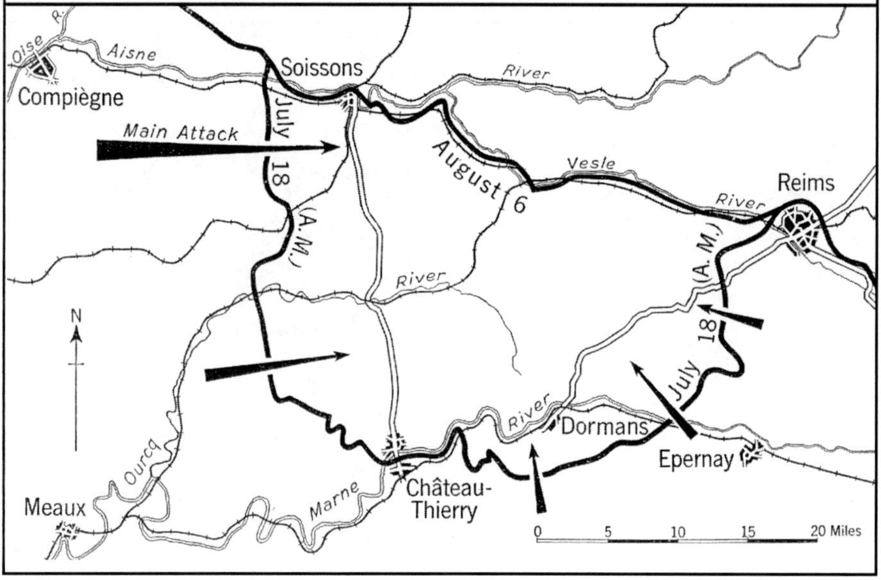

Plan of Attack of First Army, September 12, 1918

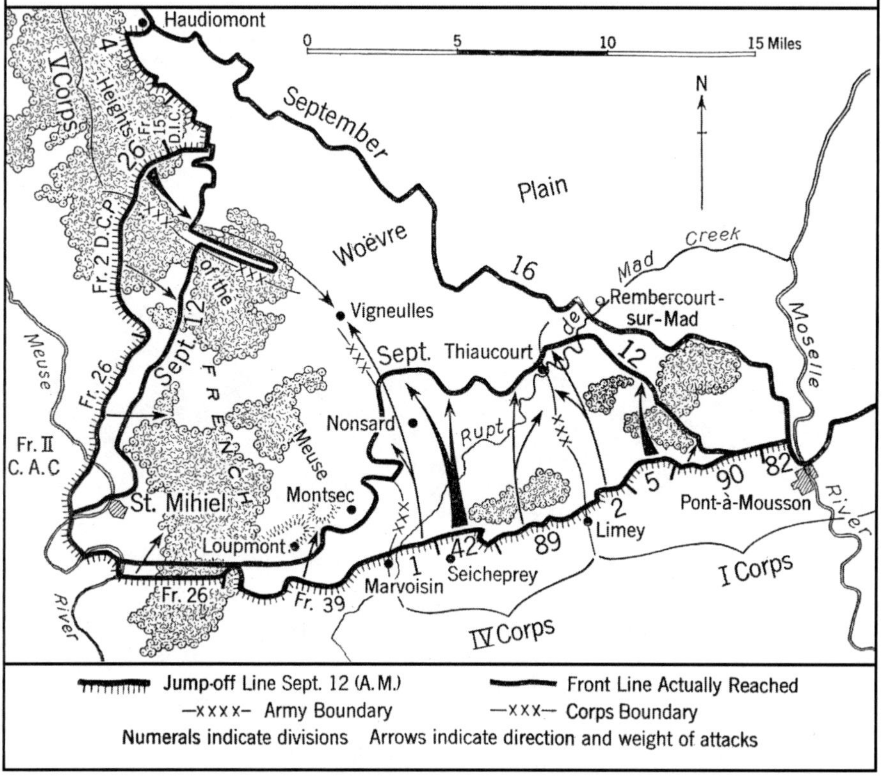

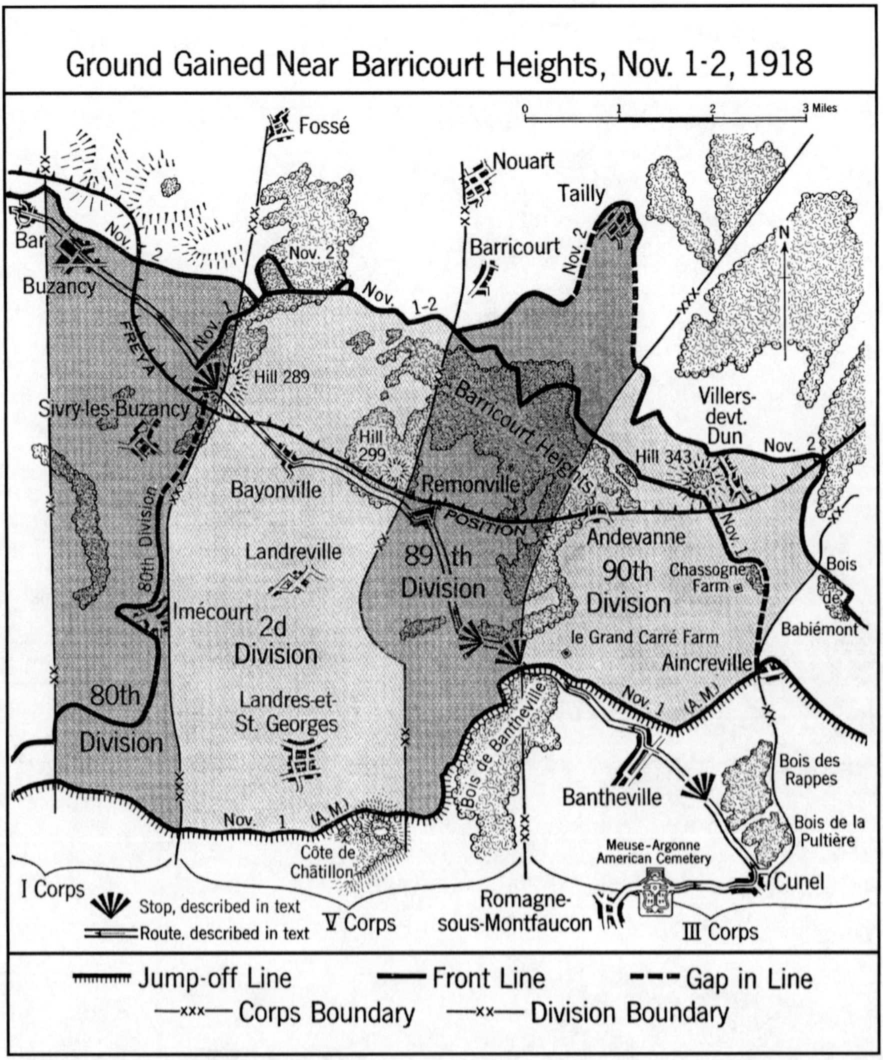
Ground Gained Near Barricourt Heights, Nov. 1-2, 1918
0 1 2 3 Miles
Fossé
Nouart
Tailly
Bar
Buzancy
Nov. 2
Nov. 1-2
Barricourt
FREYA
Nov. 1
Hill 289
Sivry-les-Buzancy
Barricourt Heights
Hill 299
Villers-devt. Dun
Hill 343
Nov. 2
Bayonville
Remonville
POSITION
Andevanne
Landreville
89th Division
90th Division
Chassogne Farm
80th Division
Imécourt
2d Division
le Grand Carré Farm
Aincreville
Bois de Babiémont
Nov. 1 (A.M.)
80th Division
Landres-et-St. Georges
Bois de Bantheville
Bantheville
Bois des Rappes
Bois de la Pultière
Nov. 1 (A.M.)
Côte de Châtillon
Meuse-Argonne American Cemetery
Cunel
I Corps
Stop, described in text
Route, described in text
V Corps
Romagne-sous-Montfaucon
III Corps
Jump-off Line
Front Line
Gap in Line
Corps Boundary
Division Boundary

Reminiscences of
Conrad S. Babcock

Introduction

My acquaintance with the memoirs of Conrad S. Babcock came slowly, curiously, and for a while without a great deal of understanding. I had come on the diary of Major General William M. Wright, the commanding general of the Eighty-ninth Division in World War I, discovered that Colonel Babcock was one of the general's four infantry colonels, decided to edit and publish the diary, and found that Babcock had written his memoirs and they were in the Hoover Institution at Palo Alto, California, on the Stanford University campus. Not desiring to travel from my home university, Indiana, I called the archivist at the Hoover and learned that they would send a copy of the memoirs but only at a rate of 100 pages a year. The manuscript was 1,100 pages in length. I accepted that, for after doing several monographs on American participation in World War I, I had begun an account of the Battle of the Meuse-Argonne, the largest, longest, and by far the most costly (26,000 men killed, tens of thousands wounded) battle in all of American history. So each year, I ordered my annual allotment, read it, and for the most part filed the pages away.

The curious part of the Babcock manuscript was that it is the only American military manuscript at the Hoover Institution. The institution's vast collections were on the subjects of war, revolution, and peace. The war portion was European, on former president Herbert Hoover's theory that Europeans started wars, and that excluded American manuscripts. I guessed that Colonel Babcock's account of his experiences from 1898 through 1918, typed by the colonel with handwritten emendations, found its way to Palo Alto because Babcock married Marion L. Eells, whose sister married the most prominent clergyman in New York City, the Reverend Henry Sloane Coffin, who could have known the founder of the Palo

Alto library. Or, a less plausible guess, Mr. Hoover, himself a voracious reader, somehow read that mass of typescript, liked it, and put it in his library.

At first, I had no sense of what had moved Babcock to draw his huge, at times photographic, picture of the change in the U.S. Army from its primitive proportions in 1898 to its European efficiencies in the final attack in the Meuse-Argonne, November 1–2, 1918 (after three failed attempts), as I was reading Babcock's manuscript piecemeal, interrupted by the difficult book on the Meuse-Argonne. Finally, I began to see that the retired colonel, writing in 1940–1941, realized that he had witnessed the drama of the American Army reforming itself, forced into massive change, belatedly and at a heavy cost in casualties. The delinquent generals survived—only two were killed—one of them Babcock's successor in the First Division who arranged his own demotion, claiming that as a general officer he was incompetent, the other in the Twenty-ninth Division who allowed his driver to take his limousine up a road under fire from German artillery. Not so the army's men; one estimate by a successful front-line battalion major was that they suffered, on average, twice the necessary casualties. Babcock saw all this, had the literary ability and the patience to set it down, and somehow it passed into a library. His narrative is the only such account I know of.

Babcock descended from eight generations of New Englanders, the first of them coming over in the great Puritan migration, settling in Portsmouth, Rhode Island, in 1642. The colonel duly described them in his memoirs. All of them put together, although he did not say that, did not see as many changes in American life as Babcock saw in his twenty years of American military affairs after 1898. But from them, who saw the rigors of the separation from Old England and making their ways in New England, the colonel obtained a feeling of where he stood in his own experiences.

The colonel's father, in a desire to do as much as he could as soon as possible, was a typical Babcock. In 1856, at age thirteen, he sailed out of New York on the clipper ship *Young America*, of which his uncle was captain and part owner. He arrived 107 days later in San Francisco just in time to observe the Vigilance Committee in charge of the city and engaged in hanging two murderers in a street in front of the fort. After three years as an officer in the Civil War, from which he emerged a major, John

Babcock enlisted in the Regular Army as a second lieutenant, ending as a brigadier general shortly before the turn of the century, spending most of those years with the 5th Cavalry in the West.

Conrad Babcock followed his father into the army, graduating from West Point in the year the war with Spain both began and, of course, ended. Because of his father's position he managed a place in the eight-thousand-man force that Major General Wesley M. Merritt took out to Manila to secure the city and the Philippine Islands themselves. When the force reached Manila Bay and bivouacked in the city the ragtag troops of the Filipinos were gathering to assist in capturing the Spanish soldiery, and then to progress to their real cause, to put in place Philippine independence. The Philippine Insurrection, as Americans described it, began shortly after Lieutenant Babcock arrived.

What Babcock observed in subsequent months and years was in part a growing U.S. Army. From after the Civil War until just before the Spanish War the army amounted to twenty-eight thousand men. It increased to 125,000, a tiny force compared with those of the great European armies, France and Germany. The U.S. Army's officers, especially the younger ones, celebrated the opportunities for promotion that their increasing troop numbers allowed and gave little or no attention to the developments in armaments in European armies and, in Germany, the development of tactics.

Babcock's memoirs show the tactical changes forced upon the U.S. Army after it met the German Army in 1918. A reader might not have expected that, for upon graduation from West Point, Babcock had wanted to be—he admired the word—a cavalryman. For a short time, so as to participate in the defense of Manila, he joined an artillery unit, but he left for the cavalry at the first opportunity. He organized a polo team that enrolled Lieutenant Jonathan M. Wainwright (the commander who would replace General MacArthur when MacArthur went to Australia during World War II). Babcock spent an exhilarating year at the French cavalry school, Saumur. When he shifted to the First Division and discovered no cavalry, he knew that artillery and machine guns had become the dominant weapons.

When he wrote the memoirs he divided them between the Old Army and the New. The first four chapters describe small actions against Filipinos and such assignments as taking a cavalry troop into the fire-destroyed city of San Francisco in 1906 or duty in the vicinity of Yuma in Arizona when border troubles were heating up with brigands and Mexican troops. The next four chapters, all for the year 1918, set out the battles of Soissons (July 18–22), St. Mihiel (September 12–16), and the immense battle of the Meuse-Argonne (September 26—November 11).

Soissons was an effort to push the German Army out of a salient. In the last of the German attacks in the offensive of 1918, which nearly ended in Allied defeat, the enemy had gotten into a salient, which meant two lines to defend instead of one, and probably would have withdrawn if two American divisions had not attacked on June 18 hoping to hasten it. One was the First Division, in which Colonel Babcock commanded the 28th Infantry Regiment, the most exposed of the division's regiments. Babcock had just taken command of the regiment and was proud of the big four-thousand-man unit, the largest he had commanded, not well trained but draft men, intelligent, willing to do whatever was necessary, presuming that if led by American officers it would follow tactically intelligent orders. Babcock's 28th Infantry did not reckon with the tactically appalling orders of the division commander, Major General Charles P. Summerall, a former artillery commander who in 1900, commanding a battery to relieve the siege of foreign residents in Peking, blew a hole through the wall of the Imperial Palace. A hero of the Old Army, Summerall knew something about gunnery but nothing about infantry, and he threw his big regiments into an attack en masse where their thick ranks, only the front lines able to fire, exposed them to machine guns and artillery. Babcock sought to apprise the general of what was happening, and Summerall concluded that the 28th under Babcock did not want to attack.

The last chapters on the New Army are about how an intelligent regimental commander, Babcock, did something about an unintelligent division commander—this when the commander-in-chief of the army in France, General Pershing, himself no tactician considered Summerall his best division commander and promoted him to corps command. Babcock spent the three weeks he had before Summerall relieved him asking officers and men what they thought went wrong at Soissons. He learned a great deal. He managed through a well-placed friend at Pershing's G.H.Q. to obtain another assignment with the Eighty-ninth Division. The Battle of St. Mihiel was too short to do much tactically. But the Meuse-Argonne was something else, and here Babcock's regiment was one of the leading regiments in the attack that drove the German Army behind the great bend of the Meuse, ensuring the end of the war.

Babcock never forgot what he learned about warfare in the twenty years from 1898 to 1918. General Summerall triumphed in the army, becoming chief of staff in 1927. Babcock remained inconspicuous until his retirement in 1937. He hoped to return to the army in 1940–1941 when at long last, after the Great Depression, it became possible to begin mobilization. The chief of staff beginning in 1939 was General George C. Marshall, a friend from the Old Army, and Babcock hoped that Marshall would bring him out of retirement. Marshall did not, and Babcock had no choice except to write his memoirs.

The memoirs held his attention, and no other officer of the Old Army did so well in describing what had happened. He died in 1950, knowing he had done his best, set it all down as he knew it. His memoirs remained unpublished until now, over a hundred years since the great change began in the U.S. Army.

One

Manila and Iloilo

Following the twentieth degree parallel of north latitude into the setting sun, the *Rio de Janeiro* passed the northern end of the island of Luzon and then, turning to the left or port as sailors once called it, steamed down the western side of the island. What a magnificent sight it was and still is. The wonderful shades of green, the lofty fern and tree clad mountain range that rises from the China Sea to heights of over seven thousand feet and extends in an almost unbroken line from the north tip of Luzon to Manila Bay. I shall never forget the thrill it gave me to gaze on that beautiful tropical and, to me, unknown fairyland and realize that on it was a war to which I was going. I didn't know that the war was already over.

As we steamed past the island of Corregidor and entered Manila Bay the first vessel of any description to meet us was a German cruiser. This big ship came alongside and then deliberately steamed completely around us, looking us over in what we all felt to be a highly disapproving manner. Of course at the time we did not know that Germans resented our capture of Manila and that Admiral Dewey had had some unpleasant experiences with them; but this German cruiser was positively insulting in the lordly way she inspected us. A little while later every man on board must have been thrilled when the outline of Dewey's ships could be seen; then, as we passed Cavite on the starboard side, the rather pathetic sight of the little Spanish vessels that had gone down at anchor came in view.

It was shortly after the thirteenth of August when we reached Manila Bay, and until news was brought on board none of us knew that General Merritt's command had captured the city of Manila, after a short, brisk engagement on August 13, one day after an armistice had been signed in Washington. Neither the Spanish nor American army and navy commanders knew of this.

1

After the then Commodore George B. Dewey brought his small squadron from Hong Kong he sank the smaller group of Spanish warships. It was not much of a contest, for the Spanish put their ships in shallow water so that they would not go down too far.

The Independent 8th Army Corps, as the Philippine Islands expedition was called, was a badly clothed and tough looking command. The enlisted men were still wearing the flannel shirts and heavy blue trousers and canvas leggings. Many of the soldiers had cut the sleeves off their shirts above the elbow. Those who had lost their gray felt campaign hats had outfitted themselves with Filipino straw hats. Neither officers nor men wore hat cords at that time. The only decently dressed outfit in the whole command was a four company battalion of the 3rd Artillery (800 strong) commanded by Major William A. Kobbé (W.P. 1862) afterwards a major general. This organization had acquired from somewhere white coats and trousers of light cotton material. I am sure they were the only American enlisted men who did not suffer all day long from the heat of the heavy blue uniforms.

Father and the rest of General Merritt's staff were living in the Spanish ex-governor general's palace, the Malacañan, on the right bank of the Pasig River. All the Spanish prisoners of war were confined to the old Walled City. I stayed with Father a day, then was ordered to join Light Battery D, 6th Artillery, commanded by my former West Point artillery instructor, Captain A. B. Dyer (W.P. 1873). The battery was quartered just east of the Walled City on Calle Nozaleda. There I found the artillery commander, Major F. C. Grugan, Captain Dyer, First Lieutenant H. L. Hawthorne who had graduated from the Naval Academy in the Class of 1882, served as a cadet engineer in the Navy until October, 1884, then been commissioned a second lieutenant in the 2nd Artillery. He was also a Medal of Honor man, won at Wounded Knee Creek, against the Indians, in 1890. The other officers were Second Lieutenant A. S. Fleming (W.P. 1895), E. D. Scott of my class, and Dr. Quinan, a volunteer medical officer.

Wounded Knee was the last battle with the Indians. The Medal of Honor, later so revered, did not amount to much for many years after its first awarding in the Civil War. Its identification with gallantry sank so low that during the Battle of Santiago in Cuba in 1898 a colonel guided a few troops across a ridge into position around the city and before returning to his command asked the colonel of the organization to recommend him for the Medal of Honor. Just before the beginning of World War I the War Department established a board to review awards of the Medal. The board lopped hundreds of recipients off the rolls and even asked recipients to return medals in their possession.

About two hundred yards east of us on Calle San Luis there was quartered what might be called a regiment of Filipino infantry. In capturing the city General Merritt had tried to keep the insurgent forces under Emilio Aguinaldo out of it as far as possible, fearing the native troops might loot the Spaniards' homes and kill those who in the past had aroused their hatred. The insurgents were occupying parts of the city when I arrived. Gradually the American military governor managed to move them all out to the outskirts of the city. As they moved and as they saw the control of the Islands slipping from them, their enthusiastic friendship for the Americans grew less and less. Many times, when we first landed, I have seen the Filipino show the American the comparative relationship then existing between the American and the Filipino and the Spaniards and the Filipino. This was done by putting the first fingers of his hands parallel and close together and then saying, with a grin, "Americano, Filipino—amigos, muchos amigos." Then he would place the ends of the index fingers together, give them a couple of jabs, scowl and say, "Español, Filipino—mucho combate." One morning the Filipino infantry regiment on Calle San Luis had to move, and just to show us how good they were, the command marched down our street then south past the east gate and drawbridge of the Walled City, then east through the suburb called Pasay and out of town.

Light battery D, 6th Artillery, had six 3.2 guns, no draft animals, only two or three little Filipino ponies about twelve hands high. The guns and their limbers and the caissons were hauled around by manpower. The command was well disciplined and instructed, and it was no fault of ours that, in appearance, there was much to be desired.

For twelve pesos, equal to six U.S. dollars, I hired an excellent Filipino boy as my personal servant. I had a large cool room in one of the well built houses on the south side of the street. The enlisted men occupied similar quarters across the street.

The Spanish prisoners, inside the Walled City of Manila, were allowed to swim in the bay across the Malacañan Drive. As the bathing hour, 4:00 p.m., approached, one could see thousands of men sitting on the south fortifications waiting for a cool dip in the bay.

There was little to do in the way of amusement, no theaters, and no parties. Of course, the Spanish officers and their families had nothing to do with us. This I often regretted as there were two pretty Spanish girls, daughters of a Spanish major, who lived not far from my quarters when I later joined G Battery of the 6th Artillery.

The one big social gathering was about 5:00 p.m., when one of our military bands played on the Luneta. Everyone who had a horse and carriage, or could hire one, drove slowly around and around the Luneta in a clockwise direction. Under the Spanish regime the only vehicles allowed to move counter-clockwise were those of the bishop of the Philippines and the governor general.

The Laneta afternoon concert appeared to be the one chance the young men had to meet their senoritas. The young women, under the eagle eye of a senora chaperone, walked demurely up and down with their caballeros or chatted with them from the family quiles, garromata or Victoria.

The Luneta was oblong in shape. From its western end the Malaccan road ran along the fortifications to the Pasig River. From its eastern end the Calle Real led through the residential district called Pasay. Oil-burning street lamps followed the perimeter of the Luneta, and in the center stood the wooden bandstand.

With the band playing, the little waves of Manila Bay running up and down the south shore of the Luneta, a gorgeous sunset ablaze over the dim outline of Corregidor, dozens of pretty girls—Filipinos, mestizos, and Spanish—strolling back and forth, it was difficult to believe that the Luneta was the official execution ground under the Spanish regime. Blindfolded, many a wretched native has stood on the gravel covered Luneta, his back to the little waves and the setting sun, four rifle armed soldier executioners facing him; while all around, save on the bay side, stood or sat in their carriages, hundreds of ladies and gentlemen, the pick of Manila society, and the native Filipino men and women for whose attempted independence the life of the insurgent was about to be forfeited in a blast of rifle fire.

Father and General Merritt left for home shortly after I arrived, and Brigadier General Elwell S. Otis (W.P. 1862) assumed command.

One day, before my father sailed, someone at headquarters gave me a copy of the following "Extraordinary Proclamation," promulgated by the Spanish governor general of the Philippine Islands on April 23, 1898.

"Spaniards:

"Between the United States and Spain hostilities have broken out. The moment has arrived to prove to the world that we possess the spirit to conquer those who, pretending to be loyal friends, take advantage of our misfortunes and abuse our hospitality, using means which civilized nations count unworthy and disreputable.

"The North American people, constituted of all the social excrescences, have exhausted our patience and provoked war with their perfidious machinations, with their acts of treachery, with their outrages against the law of nations and international conventions.

"The struggle will be short and decisive. The God of Victories will give us one as brilliant and complete as the righteousness and justice of our cause demands. Spain, which will count upon the sympathies of all the nations, will emerge triumphantly from this new test, humiliating and blasting the adventurer from those states that, without cohesion and without a history, offer to humanity only infamous traditions and the ungrateful spectacle of chambers in which appear united insolence and defamation, cowardice and cynicism.

"A squadron manned by foreigners, possessing neither instruction nor discipline, is preparing to come to this archipelago with the ruffianly intention of robbing us of all that means life, honor and liberty. Pretending to be inspired by a courage of which they are incapable, the North American seamen undertake as an enterprise capable of realization the substitution of Protestantism for the Catholic religion you profess, to treat you as tribes refactory to civilization, to take possession of your riches as if they were unacquainted with the rights of property, and to kidnap those persons whom they consider useful to man their ships or to be exploited in agricultural or industrial labor.

"Vain designs. Ridiculous boastings.

"Your indomitable bravery will suffice to frustrate the attempt to carry them into realization. You will not allow the faith you profess to be made a mock of, impious hands to be placed on the temple of the true God, the images you adore to be thrown down by unbelief. The aggressors shall not profane the tombs of your fathers; they shall not gratify their lustful passions at the cost of your wives' and daughters' honor, or appropriate the property your industry has accumulated as a provision for old age. No, they shall not perpetrate any of the crimes inspired by their wickedness and covetousness, because your valor and patriotism will suffice to punish and abase the people that, claiming to be civilized and cultivated, have exterminated the natives of North America instead of bringing to them the life of civilization and of progress.

"Filipinos, prepared for the struggle and united under the glorious Spanish flag, which is ever covered with laurels, let us fight with the conviction that victory will crown our efforts, and to the calls of our enemies let us oppose with the decision of the Christian and the patriot the cry of "Viva—Espagna!"

"Manila, 23rd April 1898,

Your General,

Basilo Augustin Davila"

In this appeal to the natives, subjects of Spain for some three hundred years, General Augustin Davila seems to have touched most of the keys to human emotions. Certainly it was not a very complimentary letter of introduction for the North Americans under Dewey or for those who followed. Among the Americans in Manila, who read this proclamation in August, 1898, there was no resentment. It was too bombastic, too filled with lies to do more than amuse the soldiers of a nation accustomed to political speakers and high pressure salesmanship. Although the formal declaration of war was not made until April 25, Congress had authorized the President to use force against Spain on April 18. General Davila's references to the "squadron manned by foreigners" indicates that he was well aware of the contemplated attack of the U.S. warships, then at Hong

Kong under Commodore Dewey, even before war was declared. Dewey's sudden appearance off Cavite was no surprise.

In the days before wireless the procedure of such attacking squadrons as Dewey's was to cut an enemy's cable connections, which the American commodore duly did for the Philippines at Hong Kong.

In October, 1898, the War Department notified the headquarters department of the Pacific, and 8th Army Corps, as the expedition was now called, that I had been assigned to Light Battery G, 6th Artillery, then in billets on Calle Real, Malate, Manila. The enlisted men were quartered in an ancient monastery next to a church. This building had a large yard about half a block square, completely surrounded by a high stone wall. This yard was our gun park. Here, day after day, this horseless light battery spent many hours at what was called "standing gun drill." One feature of that tedious performance consisted in assuming the gun in action and, under the fire of the enemy, casualties were occurring. As the theoretically wounded cannoneer fell to the ground he would shout, "Number—(giving his number) out" and his duties would be instantly taken by the proper cannoneer as designated in the *Artillery Tactics*. So routine became this procedure that many months later, on the island of Panay, in combat, one member of G Battery's gun crew actually enacted the dramatic part of the wounded gunner, calling out his number as he fell under the impact of a Mauser rifle bullet. That is the only time I have ever heard of the parade or drill theories being executed in actual combat; but, after serving eight months in G Battery under its captain, Victor H. Bridgman (W.P. 1875) one would be likely to remember a drill requirement even under the shock of a mortal wound.

The Philippines in general and Manila in particular, in 1898, were typical examples of the simple life. Railroad transportation consisted of one single-track road (English equipment) from Manila to Dagupan. Pony drawn little street cars operated from across the Bridge of Spain, through the Calle Escolta, thence out to the northern district of the city. The street railway tracks were very light rails, and the roadbed was in bad repair. Second class passengers were supposed to assist the conductor when the car ran off the track, and very frequently they could be seen carrying out this traditional service.

The word taxi had not yet come into public use in Manila, neither had automobiles. This type of service was very cheaply performed by the one or two horse, two wheeled, quilez or carromata or the four wheeled carriage. The Filipino cochero is a heartless user of horse flesh. As he drove along he clucked and shouted at his wretched little pony, jerked on the reins with almost every step of the horse and laid on the whip several times a block. When I drove with one of these gentry I made him reduce his rein and whip motions by at least half, but even this acquiescence on his part was most unwillingly performed and lasted but a moment or two unless one kept an eye on him.

Practically the entire town went to sleep during the siesta period, about eleven thirty to two thirty every afternoon. How that custom did annoy us, the Americans. With the streets filled with money spending soldiers it wasn't long before the afternoon siesta grew shorter and shorter. Now it has entirely disappeared; but for many years certain of its addicts clung to that wise and healthy tropical custom. What have the Islands gained by the change? Twelve hours a week more work. To what great and glorious future are the little brown-skinned natives and the Caucasian temporary inhabitants of those languid warm green islands now rushing?

Dinners, dances or parties of any kind were few and far between. One afternoon in October or November, I attended a tea dance on the *U.S.S. Olympia*, the flagship of George Dewey, now a four star admiral. The hero of the Battle of Manila Bay sat in a chair on the after end of the quarter deck. Dressed in full white uniform, the white haired, white mustached old gentleman looked very handsome as he watched his young officers and two or three army officers dancing with the few American and English girls then living in Manila.

One of the ensigns on the *Olympia* was the now Rear Admiral Henry Butler, retired. He took me down in his junior officers' cabin and, after a vow of deep secrecy, opened a drawer and showed me a blue flag with one white star in the center—the flag of a commodore in the navy. It was the flag flown by Commodore Dewey on the *Olympia* during the Manila battle. When the cable from Washington came announcing the promotion of the commodore and the admiral's flag was hoisted, Ensign Butler happened to be the officer designated to perform the ceremony. As the commodore pennant came down, Butler stowed it away under his coat. Up to the time he showed me his valuable historical trophy, its disappearance was a great mystery on the *Olympia*. Although I have seen Butler many times since those days, I have always forgotten to ask him what he did with the famous commodore pennant. As more than forty years have gone since this flag disappeared, I do not feel that now telling this little story is a very serious matter.

The *Olympia*, launched in the 1880s, was a small ship incomparable to the battleships of World Wars I and II. In 1921 it carried back to the United States the body of the Unknown Soldier, to be buried at Arlington. Whereupon the ship was decommissioned. It was not broken up for scrap but towed to a mooring in the Housatonic in Philadelphia. A private organization maintains it and shows occasional visitors through such portions as are maintained, including the forecastle. Brass footprints on the floor show where Dewey stood when he said to the ship's captain, "You may fire when ready, Gridley."

One day Captain Bridgman gave me permission to leave the city for a few hours and I took the morning train to Malolos, General Emilio Aguinaldo's capital. Malolos is about twenty miles from Manila. Aguinaldo was living in this small village at that time; but although I visited his headquarters (well guarded by armed sentries) I didn't see him, nor was I allowed to enter the old building then in use by the Philippine legislative body.

The town was full of Filipino armed soldiers, and their August and September friendly attitude towards Americans had greatly changed for the worse. A few days after my trip General Otis issued an order forbidding officers and enlisted men from leaving the Manila city limits without special authority.

Now, in thinking back for the cause of the Filipinos' change from almost adoration of the Americans to bitter hatred, all in the space of five months, the main cause was, in my opinion, suspicion of our intentions as to the Filipinos' part in the peacetime government of the Islands. In the autumn of 1898 no one in the Philippines, and I doubt if even President McKinley, knew what to do with the Islands, how long to keep the army there, and what, if any, part in a future government the Filipino native was to hold.

Another factor, a personal cause of unrest, was the superior attitude of the American shown towards the Filipinos of all grades. The Filipino in stature is a little fellow, his color is dark, and worse than anything else he couldn't speak English. So the soldiers looked upon them as an ignorant, lazy and childlike race, worthy of the slang names of Ka-ki-acs or Goo-goos.

2

I have always thought that had our government, in September, 1898, made up its mind to hold the Philippines, stated this definitely to Aguinaldo, promised him, and some of his leaders, important parts in the Islands' administration, and suggested that, as the country learned self-government, more and more authority would be given them, there never would have been the Insurrection period. After two years of jungle fighting, Mr. Taft established a commission form of government in which Filipinos were appointed provincial governors. If there were natives fit for such jobs in 1900 there must have been as many in 1898. Certainly fighting our army for two years hadn't taught them any civil government lessons.

A few days before Christmas, 1898, G Battery was suddenly ordered to embark on the improvised transport *Newport*, then anchored off the mouth of the Pasig River. On cascoes (big flat bottom boats) we transported our guns, caissons, ammunition and other battery property to that vessel. Brigadier General Marcus P. Miller (W.P. 1858) and staff were the other passengers, and we then learned that General Miller was to command an expedition ordered to Iloilo, island of Panay. Besides G Battery there was the 18th Infantry and the 51st Iowa National Guard on the *U.S. S. Pennsylvania*. We steamed out of Manila Bay under the escort of the navy on Christmas Eve and the next day dropped anchor off the city of Iloilo.

Being a very junior officer I was not present at any of the interviews held on board by General Miller and the Filipinos in control of Iloilo. It soon became known that when the expedition left Manila, General Otis understood that the Spanish forces that had garrisoned the island of Panay during our war with Spain were still there. In fact the Miller expedition was dispatched to relieve the Spaniards and take possession of Iloilo before the Filipinos could capture it. So when the *Newport* dropped anchor and a launch appeared with nattily dressed Filipino officers ready to offer us the courtesy of the port (except to go ashore), I imagine no one was more surprised than General Miller.

The Filipino of those days may have been unversed and inexperienced in the diplomatic art of answering a request by replying neither no nor yes, but to General Miller's announcement that his troops were to garrison Iloilo the courteous Filipino visitors postponed granting authority, with the plea that as their troops were part of Aguinaldo's army only El General Emilio himself could grant such permission. Using Dr. Phelan as his ambassador, Phelan apparently being the only person on board who could speak Spanish, General Miller kept up negotiations, but to no avail. [Henry du R. Phelan was a contract surgeon.]

Between the islands of Panay and Luzon there are today many communication waves, but in 1898 all those waves were of water. I assume the Iloilo authorities dispatched a vessel, probably a sailboat. I know that General Miller sent word of the predicament to General Otis. From December 25, 1898, until February 12, 1899, the transports of two big regiments of infantry, a light battery of artillery, and in addition three or four light cruisers or gunboats of the navy swung back and forth at their anchors as the powerful tides of the South Pacific ran through the narrow channel between the islands of Panay and Guimaras. It was reported that without Aguinaldo's consent our landing would precipitate a war with the Filipinos, and in our particular case would result in the deliberate burning of the city of Iloilo.

About a month before G Battery boarded the *Newport*, I had been appointed battery Post Exchange officer, relieving Second Lieutenant F. A. Pearce. After the first payday, when almost all the bills due the battery had been collected, I reported to Captain Bridgman that, as far as I could determine, the battery exchange had made no profit, in fact could hardly meet its indebtedness. The captain seemed to think I was mistaken, but what he should have done, and what I should have demanded had I not been so completely inexperienced in handling an exchange, even this little one, was to appoint a battery Post Exchange council and have the members carefully audit the exchange records. Nothing was done, and we went on selling bottled beer, cigars and cigarettes to the officers and enlisted men of the battery. We left Manila so suddenly and before the battery was paid for December that I had no chance to pay any of the exchange debts. After the battery was paid on the *Newport*, I sat at the pay table and found myself responsible for $897.75 in gold and silver (no paper currency was used in the Philippines) due merchants in Manila. This money I had to keep in my stateroom in my locked trunk. Some of this money was due an American beer exporting firm called the American Commercial Company managed by a smart, energetic young man named W. W. Brown. Some years later and for the rest of his life, he was called by the Americans in the Philippines the mayor of Manila. One morning in February, 1899, I heard that the former battery Post Exchange officer was going to Manila on our mail ship. Realizing that here was an opportunity to pay the battery exchange bills and get rid of all the gold and silver I was forced to keep in my trunk, I asked Pearce to take the money and pay the accounts. He agreed. So I handed him the quite heavy bag of money and the unpaid bills and was about to wish him a pleasant trip when my guardian angel put his gentle hand on my shoulder and said, "Get a receipt for the money." Taking a sheet of paper out of my pocket I wrote, "Iloilo Harbor, Feb. 1, 1899, I certify to have received from Lieut. C. S. Babcock, 1st Caval., Exchange Officer, eight hundred and ninety-seven dollars and seventy-five cents American Currency ($897.75 Gold)."

Life on the anchored transports was tedious, hot, and exasperating. We organized crews for the *Newport*'s lifeboats and fought the swift tides for exercise as we rowed along the Guimaras shore to watch the monkeys. Unarmed, a few officers were given permission to visit Iloilo, and I took advantage of it at once. Of course all the Spaniards had departed. It was reported that they had gone to join other contingents of General Aguinaldo's army in Zamboanga, island of Mindanao, or in Jolo, island of Jolo. Iloilo was a rather pretty little town. I am glad to have seen it before a large portion of it was destroyed by fire the morning our troops invaded the island of Panay.

In order to provide the troops with plenty of fresh water, obtained on the island of Guimaras, our brigade quartermaster hired from Iloilo a small steam driven vessel which was used as a water carrier. The crew consisted of an American sailor off the *Newport* as skipper, a husky Filipino sailor, two ordinary "rice dike hombres," as the hardworking field type natives were called, and a guard of two soldiers from G Battery.

When not engaged in pumping fresh water into a transport, this craft was moored to the *Newport*.

One evening, January 4, 1899, while we were at supper, a tremendous racket was heard on the water boat. Rushing up on deck, we saw two Filipinos cringing behind the wheelhouse, a bloody looking soldier lying in the scuppers aft, and far astern in the ocean came cries of "Help, help." What had happened was this. The two soldiers, armed with revolvers, were aft; the three Filipinos at supper amidships. Suddenly, without warning, the Filipino sailor drew a bolo out from under his shirt, rushed at the soldiers, hit one of them (Private Silvey) a terrible blow on the top of his head, then stabbed and knocked the other soldier (Private Kilpatrick) overboard, and then he jumped overboard.

Kilpatrick was a native of the East Side of New York City, an East River swimming expert. Long before a lifeboat could be launched from the *Newport*, he was swept toward the open sea by the swift ebb tide and lost from sight in the deepening darkness. Kilpatrick discarded his revolver, his shoes and leggings, and as the tide took him down past the naval cruiser *Brooklyn* he managed to counter the current and get hold of the cruiser's anchor chain. After that his yells produced immediate results and he was taken on board.

The bolo man we never seen again, but it was rumored on shore that he had been able to swim ashore, a feat believed impossible at that particular state of the tide.

Perhaps the most remarkable feature of the whole affair was the ultimate recovery of the wounded soldier, Silvey. Our battery surgeon, Dr. Phelan, told me that the man's head was split from right to left temple with parts of the brain protruding. Phelan trepanned the skull in an improvised operating room in the ship's mess hall. A few weeks later I saw Silvey walking around before going off on a sick leave to Manila.

The water boat captain was not on board when the attempted murder took place and although some excited sailors beat up the two Filipinos before they could be stopped, these badly scared little men proved they had taken no active part in the mutiny, although I am sure they knew what the native sailor intended doing.

The water boat sailor captain was an old tar off the *Newport*. Probably in all his long seafaring life this was his first command, and the pride that gleamed in his eye over that wretched little tub was beautiful to behold, rather pathetic too. He kept his ship scrubbed and polished like a battleship. One day I happened to make a trip on this boat from the *Newport* to the *Pennsylvania* occupied by the 51st Infantry, Iowa National Guard. This regiment had been on board the *Pennsylvania* at that time for over sixty days I believe. Except for a few individuals no one had put foot on dry land since leaving San Francisco.

There were, of course, no women on board, and a view of the ship's decks was a sight into the then unknown nudist colony of today—less the women. Men strolled about clad in just their birthday suits. Occasionally some artistic National Guard soldier wore a hat and a stiff white collar (I have no idea where the collar came from, probably borrowed from an officer) to emphasize his lack of dress.

Well, on the particular day we came alongside the ship shortly after the men's dinner. The kitchen police were dumping the remains of a regimental meal into a huge iron tub that swung out from the ship's side and, at that time, hung right over the little water boat. I noticed a few soldiers looking down on us from the kitchen deck, and realizing the temptation and the opportunity I hastily walked forward just in time to escape a perfect Niagara of swill that fell on the immaculate deck of our vessel. The rage of the water boat captain was awe inspiring. The language of this postgraduate forecastle orator of steam vessels and windjammers was colossal. While I deeply sympathized with our skipper, darned if I could help laughing.

The Miller expedition, now forgotten, showed the reluctance with which the American Army in the Islands faced up to the Philippine Insurrection. Given Aguinaldo's hopes and the total unpreparedness of the Islands for self-government, what nation other than the United States would have kept Miller's force swinging at anchor for weeks on end because the junior Filipino officers in Iloilo could not obtain Aguinaldo's permission to welcome the Americans ashore? The reader will see mention of the cruiser *U.S.S. Brooklyn,* at that time a well known ship of the U.S. Navy, swinging with the transports in the channel between Panay and Guimaras, before the city of Iloilo.

The *Brooklyn* was a part of the celebrated ABCD squadron appropriated by Congress in 1880, the *Atlanta, Brooklyn, Chicago,* all cruisers,

and the dispatch boat *Dolphin*, the first armored ships of "the new navy," so much remarked by Americans who followed with such battleships as the *Maine*, destroyed in Havana harbor in 1898, and the *Oregon* (1890), which remained in commission until 1941. As for the experience of men aboard the *Pennsylvania* in 1898–99, see the testimony of a young citizen of Red Oak, Iowa, a member of the Iowa Guard regiment, Lloyd D. Ross, "History of Company 'M', . . . " (State Historical Society of Iowa, Des Moines).

On the twenty-third of January, 1899, headquarters 1st Separate Brigade, 8th Army Corps (General Miller's command) presented me with a War Department order transferring me from the 6th U.S. Artillery to the 1st Cavalry, Troop C, then stationed at Fort Robinson, Nebraska. I was delighted to get into the cavalry: I had applied for it upon graduation from West Point, and again upon reaching the Philippines. For some unknown reason, probably the carelessness of some clerk in the adjutant general's department in Washington, my date of rank as an officer had been changed from April 26, 1898, to September 27, 1898. That meant that dozens of men commissioned from civil life in the army, a month or two after my class, would now rank me. The small steamer that occasionally brought us mail was expected in about two weeks. General Miller granted me authority to go to Manila on that vessel for the purpose of sending a cablegram to my father, then adjutant general of the department of California, asking him to get the date of my cavalry commission straightened out. Father had to go to Washington to clear the red tape and have the new commission re-dated. I should have offered to reimburse him for this expense but being just an unthinking lieutenant interested principally in my own affairs it never occurred to me.

The mail boat returned to Manila on February 6, 1899. When the port boarding officer met the vessel we heard the news of the outbreak of the Philippine Insurrection under Emilio Aguinaldo.

West Point was a club, no doubt about it. The question that needed asking, and almost never was, concerned whether its coziness, symbolized with the de rigueur uniform of approximately the War of 1812 and the courses in military duties taught at "the Point," had any importance in warfare even in 1898, not to mention the coming World War I and

that unimaginable year 1918 when the Americans encountered the warfare of the German Army, the best army in Europe, for that matter the world, at that time.

Babcock was different from his fellow graduates of the Point, perhaps because of the family background, the experiences of his father, and behind them the other generations of Babcocks going back near the founding of the first English settlement. He had an independent streak, not yet in evidence at the end of his first Philippine tour. He found himself in the artillery at the outset of this tour, then received a transfer to the cavalry. The artillery was one of the most important parts of the army in 1918, not recognized as such for a few precious months but essential at the end. Throughout the years until real war engulfed his country Babcock like so many cavalrymen, as they described themselves, thought horses were the very core of the army. This delusion was part of all armies. In August, 1914, the first photographs of the German Army showed the lancers riding horses, appropriately, through the Tiergarten. The French Army, so admired in the late 1890s and the years until the First War, preened itself on the abilities of officers trained at its cavalry school, Saumur. Babcock spent a year studying, he would have put it, at Saumur. In the same years in which the machine gun, used in a primitive model in the Philippines early in the Insurrection, was being perfected, Saumur was flourishing, no connection evident (even to Babcock) between horses and machine guns. West Point, incidentally, continued with horses long after 1914–18 showed them defenseless to machine guns, and the present writer, teaching at the Point in 1987–88, found himself with an office in a drafty, uncomfortably so, building fairly recently converted from a horse barn. Babcock admired what his fellows admired and came away from it all as slowly as they but once reality confronted him in 1918 he spoke no more of this military anachronism. He went over to the New Army in an admirable hurry.

Two

Insurrection

Ever since the occupancy of Manila in August by the expeditionary force there had been friction between the Americans and the Filipinos over the question as to what were the outer limits of the American lines. Deliberate encroachments upon the lines were said to have been made by the Filipinos in December and January when junior Filipino officers invaded territory their superiors had ordered evacuated. About January 20, 1899, part of the 1st Nebraska National Guard Regiment had moved to some high ground beyond the Santa Mesa racetrack in the northern suburbs of Manila. On February 2 a detachment of the Filipinos, Colonel San Miguel's troops, deliberately came inside the American lines and took possession of a little barrio of houses in front of the American outposts. General Arthur MacArthur, commander of the division north of the Pasig River, sent one of his officers with a personal note of protest to San Miguel saying, "From this date, if the line is crossed by your men with arms in their hands, they must be regarded as subject to such action as I deem necessary." Two nights later, about 8:30 p.m., February 4, four Filipinos refused to obey the challenge "Halt," as they were advancing toward the little barrio and a Nebraska private soldier fired the shot that soon after started an engagement all around Manila.

General Arthur MacArthur was the father of General Douglas MacArthur. He succeeded General Otis to command of U.S. forces in the Islands.

This is the American version of the outbreak, as compiled from the reports of the military authorities in Manila. In Congress some three years later it was charged in the Senate that the American authorities in Manila had deliberately brought on the war. The unratified Spanish-American peace treaty had been before the Senate since January 4, 1899. On the sixth of February the vote was to be taken. There was some doubt as to whether the two-thirds vote necessary to ratify would be secured. Senator Thomas H. Patterson of Colorado on May 26, 1902 (to quote the *Congressional Record*), said, "The treaty had to be ratified and there was no way to bring that about except by precipitating the battle of February 4 or 5, and it was precipitated. It was another case of American duplicity. This time it was practiced upon the American Senate and the American people, and not alone upon the Filipinos, as had so often been the case before."

1

My expensive cablegram dispatched, I rushed up to headquarters and endeavored to get the adjutant general, Thomas H. Barry (W.P. 1877), to let me join or be attached to the 4th Cavalry, then somewhere along the active front line. But he wouldn't do it. He said as I really belonged to Troop C, 1st Cavalry, in Nebraska, I either ought to be sent there or remain with Battery G, 6th Artillery. Lieutenant Colonel Barry was a rough spoken old staff officer, and the best I could get out of him was permission to join the 3rd Artillery (four big coast artillery companies armed and equipped as infantry) until a ship was ready to return to Iloilo.

I found the command in line of battle near Calcoocán. The enemy in our front was about one thousand yards away across a dry rice field. The entire battalion, some eight hundred men, had dug and was occupying lying down shelter trenches. Major Kobbé, commanding, had a wall tent about one hundred yards behind the center of the line. The company officers just sat on the ground behind their entrenched commands, and at night slept under bushes near at hand. I am sure the 3rd Artillery were expert seacoast troops but they appeared to know very little about entrenching infantry or occupying a defensive position.

My company commander was Second Lieutenant Lloyd England (W.P. 1896), a friendly, jolly little man. Just before dark, the afternoon I reported, Major Kobbé sent for all the officers. He told us it was reliably reported in

Manila that Aguinaldo would attack us sometime that night. That there were no supporting troops behind us, and that we must stand fast at all costs. Furthermore, the Filipino attack would probably be made with the bolo.

You may be sure that was interesting and exciting news. At this early period of the Philippine Insurrection the bolo man and his long heavy bolo or knife was a new type of warrior to the American soldier. One could lie awake at night and visualize the stealthy approach of a horde of naked men, each man gripping the carabao handle of a razor sharp two foot long heavy knife. Suddenly the crouching mass stands erect and then, with maniacal yells, the savage bolo men were upon you.

Returning to the company, England assembled his command and from the top of a commissary box he gave what I believe a football coach calls a "pep talk." It was a humdinger. I can't remember much of it, but I do remember his telling the men that they stood between the bolo men and the women and children in Manila. I assumed he meant American women and children, and that impressed me as when I was last stationed in Manila, in December, there were no American children and only a few women. Under no circumstances were we to retreat. If men on your right and left are killed, you must stand fast. He also explained that the Filipinos would probably attack with the bolo but that fact must not cause us to retreat. It was a great talk, but by the time it was over I fear the company that had only once been under fire was a bit jittery.

Before dark the battalion sent out a number of Cossack posts (four men to a post) under Second Lieutenant Henry M. Boutelle (W.P. 1898). There were probably a hundred men in all and they were posted over two hundred yards to our front. To our left was the 20th Kansas National Guard Regiment commanded by Colonel Frederick Funston, a typical soldier of fortune, later to be celebrated as the man who captured Aguinaldo. To the right was, I believe, the 10th Pennsylvania National Guard Regiment. From there on the American line extended clear around Manila to the bay.

About 9:00 p.m. I was lying on a blanket in rear of my platoon trenches when suddenly out in front I heard shouts, the sounds of men running, and the rattle of their equipment as some of them fell over the little dike walls that covered the dry rice field. Of course, the soldiers heard the uproar. They were getting up and poking their rifles over the low embankment. All along the line could be heard the clang and bang of the Krag rifle bolts as the rifles were loaded from the hinged magazine chambers.

England and I went up and down the line, cautioning the men not to fire until the outposts were in. I was sure some excited soldier would fire and that might have started a burst of rifle fire that could easily have wiped out the outpost that was at the moment apparently coming back to our line in great disorder.

After all that bolo talk I had visions of each member of the outpost being ridden in by an Aguinaldo bolo man. Presently, out of the darkness, a wildly running soldier hit the top of the trench bank and fell over it right in front of me. "What's the matter with you, what happened out there?" I asked. Between gasps for breath he said he had been posted as a sentinel in front of his three companions. It was very dark and quiet and soon he thought the other members of his Cossack post had left him all alone. Of course the real answer was fright.

Actually not a Filipino had been seen and only a shot or two fired by the enemy. Yet the entire outpost of the 3rd Artillery ran in. Lieutenant Boutele gathered them up and took them out again; but, believe it or not, about a half hour later, as a few bullets from the direction of the insurgents whined over our line, in they came again. This time, after order had been restored, we were ordered to fire a couple of company volleys. The Filipinos must have been astonished to hear the loud commands and the crash of the rifles as our battalion fired by company, followed by the 20th Kansas and the 10th Pennsylvania. Even some naval vessel out in the northwest section of the bay fired a cannon shot. We were certainly inexperienced warriors. After the volley firing Boutelle took the outpost out again, but a little later in they came again. After the noise and excitement had subsided we heard far out in front the tired and disgusted voice of Boutelle saying, "Will somebody please send that damned outpost out to me." I heard laughter along the line, men began to guy the members of the outpost and when it rejoined Boutelle this time it remained the rest of the night. The gallant Boutelle was killed in November while serving with the Macabebe Scouts.

The Macabebe people proved willing to recruit to the American side. Eighty of them assisted in capture of the Filipino leader Aguinaldo in 1901.

This outpost episode taught me an important lesson in handling American soldiers: never harangue them, just announce the fact that we or the enemy will attack.

A few days later the 1st Tennessee National Guard Infantry sailed for Iloilo and I had to go back to G Battery. Well do I remember the short voyage with that happy-go-lucky outfit. I knew them well at Camp Merritt in San Francisco. Later they were moved into a ravine just west of the end of the Union Street cable car line in the Presidio. This ravine for many years thereafter was called Tennessee Hollow. This regiment was the descendant of the 1st Tennessee Confederate Infantry of Civil War days. The commanding officer was an ex-Confederate, Colonel Gracie; many of the members were the sons or grandsons of former Tennessee Confederates. A courageous, hilarious, wild outfit. The last National Guard regiment to be mustered out of the service in 1899.

Several contingents went out to Manila in the summer of 1898, General Merritt sailing with the third commanded by Brigadier General E. S. Otis. A total of 407 officers and 10,437 men reached Manila by the time the war ended. Two contingents arrived afterward. The one with Second Lieutenant Babcock left San Francisco on July 23-29 with 1,735 troops. It was under command of Brigadier General Harrison Gray Otis, owner of the *Los Angeles Times*, not to confuse with General E. S. Otis.

It was late in the evening of February 10, 1899, before our ship reached Iloilo. As we approached the city, one of the warships turned a searchlight on us. The transport captain had blast after blast blown to signify that the light was blinding him. Bringing a ship filled with soldiers into a strange harbor was difficult enough, without some fool warship's commander keeping a powerful searchlight on our ship until we were almost ready to anchor. Our skipper paced up and down the bridge calling on the Lord to sink the Navy.

Our arrival brought General Miller the first news of the native rebellion against the American rule, and orders to take Iloilo. Ever since Christmas the First Separate Brigade had growled and sweated on those hot transports. General Miller had two or three staff officers. The general himself spent many hours daily playing chess with the fourth mate of the *Newport*. If any plans or orders looking to a sudden landing were prepared during those idle days I never saw or heard of them.

Nowadays such an expedition would have jammed the *Newport* with general staff officers and other types of clerical warriors. Maps, plans, and reams of typewritten orders would have filled every officer's dispatch case and pockets. But while the Marines, later followed by the infantry, were going ashore in ships: boats, our guns and caissons were slowly hoisted out of the hold of the freight deck, Iloilo was burning like a four-alarm fire. I, a second lieutenant and the junior officer on board, was by General Miller's order down in the dining saloon trying to enlarge a little map of Iloilo and the neighboring territory. The command disembarked without serious opposition. Had there been any, that wretched map made by me at the eleventh hour and fifty-ninth minute could never have been used to place the line of battle on the terrain of victory.

At the close of the Spanish-American War the Astor Battery seems to have had sufficient political influence to have its members returned to the United States, leaving the little one-pounders in Manila. Some of these guns went with us to Iloilo. Ostheim, the senior lieutenant, was given command of an improvised battery of these guns and one 45-caliber brass revolving rifle machine gun, which he organized on the *Newport*. His assistant, at the time the brigade occupied Iloilo, Molo, and Jaro, was Second Lieutenant Frank C. Bolles, 18th Infantry (W.P. 1895). Bolles, now a retired major general, was wounded in the leg in the capture of Jaro, and I with my two 3.2-inch guns and caissons was ordered to Jaro to report to Lieutenant Ostheim.

Jaro, three miles from Iloilo, was a picturesque little village built along the right or south bank of the Jaro River. Except for a few Chinese, it was completely deserted. From the well built types of tropical houses, it was apparent that well to do Spaniards or natives had lived there. Ostheim's command was quartered in an abandoned monastery facing the town plaza. The headquarters of the 18th Infantry and some of the companies lived in the town, but most of the regiment was used to man their fortifications built around the town and down the right bank of the Jaro River, where they connected with the 1st Tennessee Infantry. Opposite the American outpost line, the insurrectos had an entrenched line; the no-man's-land in-between averaged almost four hundred yards, but the

Filipinos were near enough to the town to shoot into the plaza with their Mauser or Remington rifles.

By rustling around we acquired eight humpbacked native cattle, several ponies, and a two-wheeled cart with a plaited fiber cover. Dr. Phelan used the cart as an ambulance.

Of the many means used by American artillery since colonial days to move their guns on the march or in battle, I am sure none has been more novel than the gun teams we improvised for my platoon. With the regulation harness we hitched four cattle to each gun. The driver of the lead team sat on a McClellan saddle cinched to the near leader. By ropes leading to rings in the nose of each beast the rider controlled his team. The wheel team was driven by a soldier seated on the limber chest of the gun, his means of communication also being the nose ring and rope. Under constant cussing and urging this steer battery could make, perhaps, two miles an hour, but if as once happened the guns were brought into action where the grass was thick and green, the motive power would stop and graze under short range enemy rifle fire in spite of all our efforts to make them realize how dangerous we thought it was.

2

During the time I was ashore on the island of Panay, General Miller's command had three pretty good fights with the insurgents. In addition a battery sergeant and I came within an ace of being killed or captured while out hunting for ponies far beyond our outpost line.

While sniping and desultory firing went on daily, the first real action of my military career occurred the day following my arrival in Jaro, and before our animal gun teams had been acquired. On February 14, 1899, I was ordered to report to Major Charles Keller (W.P. 1865), 18th Infantry, with the brass Gatling gun and its crew. At the assembly point I found A Company, 18th Infantry, and a platoon of the command of First Lieutenant B. H. Wells (W.P. 1894). Wells is now a major general retired.

In a few moments Major Keller rode up on a little pony, followed by a trumpeter on foot. At the major's direction we started behind the infantry pulling the Gatling gun, which was coupled to its limber. Major Keller led the reconnaissance up the road along the right bank of the Jaro River.

After passing the sandbagged outpost position the infantry deployed as skirmishers to the right and left of the road. The Gatling gun, uncoupled from its limber, we pushed muzzle foremost down the road, the limber being pulled behind it. Then came Major Keller on his pony and his orderly trumpeter.

A few hundred yards beyond our outpost position the insurgents opened quite a heavy fire. At least it appeared so to me, walking down that open road in my first engagement. The whine of the Mauser bullets and the louder 45-caliber Remingtons made me feel like lying down in the dirt of that road or seeking cover behind the many trees and thick brush that lined it. I glanced back at the fat little major just in time to see his trumpeter scurrying for shelter, and returning as hastily under a scornful tongue lashing from the gallant Keller. No young officer could have had a better example of courage and complete disregard of rifle fire than was shown to me, time after time, by Keller as we made that two mile reconnaissance into the enemy territory.

For the Gatling gun ammunition, there were two large round cartridge magazine drums. Each one held one hundred 45-caliber cartridges. The gun was fired by placing a magazine in the loading slot on top of the brass barrel containing the steel barrels, and then turning a handle that operated the loading, the firing pin, the shell ejector, and the revolution of the barrels. When that old Gatling gun got going, the banging of the exploding cartridges and the crashing of the heavy lead bullets, as they flew through bamboo shacks, bushes and trees, was very exciting; and how it scared the enemy. The Gatling or machine gun was the newest idea in modern weapons at this time. Only seven months before, at Santiago, Cuba, First Lieutenant John H. Parker (W.P. 1892), Gatling Gun Parker, had made himself and the Gatling gun famous. I am sure that my brass Gatling gun was the first one ever fired on the island of Panay, possibly anywhere in the Philippines up to that time.

This short discussion of the Gatling gun shows how a revolutionary development—it was nothing less—can enter and leave the minds of those who should be most concerned. The obvious reason why the Gatling machine gun should have been fixated in Babcock's mind was its future importance in World War I, when it was one of the three

dominant weapons and hence dominated the tactics of the U.S. Army (the other weapons being artillery and poison gas) .

The Filipino soldier is no coward. Some of them are exceptionally courageous, spectacularly so at times. An insurrecto of this type gave an exhibition of nerve, coupled with great luck, during this engagement. We were pushing the gun forward on the road; the infantry was making slow progress through the fields, bamboo groves, brush and trees. Neither we nor the enemy were firing at the moment. Suddenly, not twenty feet away from behind some thick brush on the side of the road, appeared a rifle armed insurrecto. For a fraction of a second he stood there, apparently undecided to fire at us or run. Then he ran through the brush to our right like a scared rabbit. It happened that part of Wells's command was crossing an open field at that time. The men saw the running Filipino and opened a hot fire at less than fifty yards. Although that Filipino ran along the entire front of a line of probably thirty infantrymen, and made no effort to turn to his left and increase the distance, he apparently wasn't hit. I believe he had intended killing one or more members of the group on the road. Then at the last second his nerve deserted him. For that I am still most grateful. Had he fired from ambush at twenty feet, even as wretched marksman as was the average Filipino, he could not have missed at least one of us.

Our casualties, all in the infantry, were one killed and one wounded. A small loss when one considered the amount of firing that we received during the reconnaissance.

It was a Tennessee soldier that brought on the next Jaro engagement. Feeling adventuresome, this wild young private had strolled over into Jaro from Iloilo, or wherever his company was stationed, just to look us and the insurrectos over. Wandering out to the 18th Infantry outpost line, across the Jaro River, he spied an insurgent flag flying from a pole near one of their outpost positions some five hundred yards away across a thick growth of sugar cane. Although it is hard to believe, he stole that flag, got back unhurt, and brought on such a heavy Filipino rifle fire that three companies of the 18th Infantry and the fourth section (one gun) of my 3.2-inch battery was ordered out to attack the enemy. Major Keller, who I was told was out foraging in some of the abandoned vegetable gardens near the river, took charge, and armed with a handkerchief full of some vegetables he advanced his command to within short range of the insurgent main line and then fell back. I took the cattle drawn gun to within seven hundred and fifty yards of the enemy's front line, and it was while we were crossing a field of lush green grass that my fleet gun team decided to graze. The enemy took full advantage of it, without hitting anything but the gun and caisson. We pulled and whipped the beasts in our effort to get out of that open field, and then began firing shells and shrapnel. In spite of the fact that I could see the shells striking the enemy's trenches and the shrapnel bursting in front of them, after each artillery shot one could see the insurgents' straw hats come up, followed by a heavy but badly aimed rifle fire. It must be remembered that the indirect, or behind a hill, method of artillery firing was still many years off. Our guns were fired by sighting directly at a visible enemy.

The last action in which I took part on the island of Panay occurred on March 16, 1899. It was called the Battle of Jaro River. Most if not all of the 18th Infantry participated, also Lieutenant Ostheim's entire battery, escorted by a platoon from the 1st Tennessee Infantry. I don't know what objective was desired. We advanced several hundred yards and the infantry and artillery kept up a heavy fire. About dark, the entire command returned to Jaro or the entrenched positions.

One incident that amused as well as impressed me during this battle was the sight of the commanding officer of the 18th Infantry, Colonel David D. Van Valzah (1861), going into action behind a platoon of his big regiment. The platoon in question was advancing by rushes. At the command of the platoon commander the men would fire, then rise and run forward thirty or forty yards, then at command down they would go. Right behind the line came the old colonel (a Civil War veteran) rising, running forward, falling, again and again. Looking back over these many years I realize that even then, as a very young second lieutenant, I knew that the colonel was not acting as the commanding officer of a regiment in action. But it was a gallant spectacle, one that put courage into the most timid heart. I suppose when the courageous old gentleman got under fire he forgot all about being a colonel. Perhaps, in his mind, he was again a lieutenant in the Civil War, advancing towards the Confederates.

What is the real value of regimental, brigade, and division commanders in action? It is a debatable subject. In our army, up to and including the

Spanish-American War, the higher commanders actually led their troops into action, or were so near the actual firing line that their personal leadership was known and felt. The morale value of a courageous and skillful commander under these circumstances is priceless. With the arrival of the American Expeditionary Forces in France in 1917 our army adopted the trench or fortress warfare of the French Army. Leadership, actual physical leadership in action, rarely was exercised by any commander above that of the battalion. By telephone or runner from the depths of a deep dugout, most regimental, brigade, and all division and corps commanders "led" their troops into action. Of course, a regimental commander should not narrow his field of command and observation to a platoon or company, but, even there, in my opinion he exercises far more of that inexplicable emergency uplift called leadership than any dugout commander can ever give his fighting soldiers.

The casualties for the entire command were one killed and fifteen wounded, I believe. This was another example of a useless casualty list, even if small, a huge expenditure of ammunition, and no permanent gains.

General Miller recommended me for a brevet commission as first lieutenant. Up to this time gallantry in action or distinguished service was rewarded by brevet rank, but during the Philippine Insurrection for some unknown reason no one so recommended received the award. After the Great War these old brevet recommendations were turned into Silver Star citations.

After my platoon guns had been equipped with the little hump-backed native cattle, a battery sergeant and myself mounted on ponies saddled with the regulation saddles and bridles undertook to ride cross country from Jaro to Molo, hoping to find a few extra ponies. Molo is about two miles southwest of Jaro, and lies between the sea and the Iloilo River. Our map showed that there was a bridge over the Iloilo River near Molo and there were not supposed to be any insurgents in that direction. The trip was made principally as a chance to see the country, possibly find a pony or two and as an adventure not likely to have any element of danger. In fact we thought the 1st Tennessee Infantry held Molo. After riding through one small collection of native shacks where I noticed three or four unfriendly looking natives, we reached the Iloilo River. Riding along its bank on a high narrow embankment we came to the only bridge over that stream. It was impassable, due as I now remember to the removal of the plank flooring.

We were leisurely riding home across a wide dry field when all of a sudden the notes of a bugle, apparently coming from a spot about one hundred yards to our front, were heard. Scarcely had the last note died away when up jumped a line of a dozen or more men; up came their guns and a fairly good volley was fired at us. I was so surprised and so scared and felt so conspicuous sitting high in the air on my little pony, that without thinking I jumped off the pony and got behind him, or rather turned him around so he was between me and the insurgents. The sergeant followed suit. Of course what I should have done was to remain mounted and ridden rapidly out of range. With the enemy's bullets zipping by or kicking up the dirt all around us I realized we couldn't stay there. Keeping the ponies between us and the Filipinos we led them as fast as possible back to a long line of bamboo trees. With the armed Filipinos in full chase, firing as they came, we finally got under cover and at the same time got into the worst swamp I ever struggled through. The ponies sank to their bellies and we to our knees, but fortunately the enemy gave up the pursuit due either to the swamp or for fear of coming within range of our revolvers. Finally we arrived, once more, at the Iloilo River below the destroyed bridge and directly across from the town of Molo. The high bank on the far side was lined with natives attracted there by the heavy firing that we had just escaped and not seeing any American uniforms among them I rather expected to be fired on by some of them, or to be captured if we could cross. We had no intention of trying that terrible swamp again or the known enemy on its other side, so I decided to cross. The river was about 250 feet across and had a swift current. I knew the ponies couldn't swim with us on their backs and having had no experience with them before, wasn't any too certain they could make it with saddles on and holding onto the saddle pommels.

While the sergeant and I were discussing the matter, as well as watching for the reappearance of our ambushing friends, there appeared a Filipino suffering from what may have been leprosy. His whole upper jaw and nose were missing. I have never seen a more repulsive sight nor welcomed a more necessary friend. By grunts and signs he led us up the river a short distance, pulled an outrigger canoe out of the bushes. We unsaddled the ponies, and as our poor wretched friend paddled us over the river the two ponies swam behind at the end of their halter shanks, held by two dirty and tired young soldiers as ever escaped from a badly managed ambush and worse retreat.

3

Before my troop left the town of Tayabas, Mr. William H. Taft, who had been appointed by President McKinley the head of the U.S. Philippine Commission, arrived in our province to initiate the establishment of civil government. He toured the Islands with a huge party, among those who visited the town of Tayabas were Mrs. Taft, Miss Helen and Robert Taft, Commissioners Dean C. Worcester, Luke E. Wright, Henry C. Ide, Bernard C. Moses, Mr. Fred W. Carpenter (Taft's secretary), and a raft of ex-insurgents now hot on the trail of lucrative political jobs.

The vast majority of the inhabitants of the town of Tayabas were sick of the disturbed conditions of affairs. They wanted to cooperate with an American civil government. Elaborate bamboo arches of welcome were erected over the road from Lucena and the streets through which Mr. Taft would enter Tayabas. The night of their arrival a grand *baile* (dance) was given. Of course, we danced the great square dance (two couples on each of the four sides) the Rigadoon. Mr. Taft, a colossal figure in a white sack suit, danced opposite to me with a pretty little Filipino senorita whose head barely reached his elbow.

None of the commissioners could equal Mr. Taft in weight or waist measurement, but they were all tall, and as they got out of the carriages that had brought them from Lucena, I heard many of the little Filipinos exclaim *muy grande*.

On July 4, 1901, Mr. Taft became the first American governor general of the Philippine Islands; Judge Ide headed the judicial department, Mr. Worcester the interior department, Mr. Moses the department of education, and Mr. Wright the department of agriculture.

The civil rule of the army, except on the island of Mindanao, was over. All the army had to do was to continue the pacification of the Islands, kill and get killed, and make Mr. Taft's rules and regulations really work. Major General Adna R. Chaffee commanded the division of the Philippines, as it was now called, and Brigadier General Wade commanded the department of southern Luzon.

With the authority of the division commander army officers were appointed provost courts for the trial, without jury, of natives. These provost courts had jurisdiction over a long list of minor offenses and could, if my recollection is correct, sentence a convicted native to a maximum of one year in Bilibid, the Manila prison.

My troop commander held one of these jobs for a time, and up in the town of Lucban (about nine miles north of Tayabas) where Troop A was then stationed my old friend Sean Wright was the august judge. Once I spent several days in Lucban while on a reconnaissance with a large detachment of my troop. Lieutenant Wright held court every morning and at his invitation I attended a session, feeling certain that the primitive temple of justice and the bewildered and ignorant petty offender would be forgotten in observing the impeccable courtesy of the Kentucky judge, his fatherly interest in the family life of the native sinner, and the type of offenses which would be graphically presented to the judge through three languages, Tagalo, Spanish, English.

The guards and court attaches had been detailed from Troop A with these at their proper posts, Judge Wright entered, seated himself behind the bar of justice, and, in the soft accents of a southern gentleman, requested the first prisoner be brought before him.

The door was opened by a cavalry sergeant who said, "Bring in Miguel Pilar." In the hall a voice said, "Hi, Pilar, alles pronto hombre, pronto." In came Pilar. His head and feet bare, Pilar stood in soiled white cotton trousers, a collarless sort of white shirt with the shirt tails worn outside the upper part of the trousers—*camisa exterior* it was called. His wide brimmed straw hat held in his hands, while, with prehensile toes, he scraped up little piles of dust on the stone floor or sorted out broken bits of stone.

Pilar was accused of stealing a carabao from Francisco Montez, time and place being stated. What follows is not accurate; it only represents the type of provost court trial I heard.

Through the spoken word of three languages, the gist of this offense against provincial peace was transmitted to Pilar.

Was he guilty or not guilty?

Pilar, having been told that that meant had he or had he not stolen the carabao from Montez, replied in pathetic Tagalo, which when sifted through Spanish turned up in English to be, "No, Senor, I never stole anything. I am very poor and have many children."

Then came a series of native witnesses, for and against, and finally the judge had Pilar up for questioning before coming to a finding.

"How old are you, Pilar?"

"I do not know, perhaps thirty, senor."

"Have you a father and mother?"

"No Senor, both are dead."

"What did they die of, Pilar?"

"Fever and smallpox, senor."

With these pertinent facts discovered, Judge Wright went into the home life of the culprit's grandparents, the peso value of carabaos, the yield of a coconut tree, and what Mrs. Pilar and the children were doing.

Then the kind-hearted judge, who apparently couldn't bring himself to announce a guilty sentence, would return Pilar to his cell and call for the next victim. It seemed possible that Wright's prisoners might never be sentenced under his system—just tried every day or two. They could go on, week after week, eating soldiers' food and growing fat waiting to be condemned.

The Tayabas visit of the American commission, however, had no effect upon the activities of the native guerrilla bands. A sub-post of Lucena was the town of Pagbilao about five miles northeast, Pagbilao built at the mouth of a mountain stream emptying into Pagbilao Bay, in turn a part of the Bay of Tayas.

A detachment of Troop L. under a sergeant garrisoned the town. Taking advantage of market day and a bit of carelessness on the part of the detachment, which had evidently decided there was no enemy in the vicinity, a band of guerrillas came into town, almost captured the cavalrymen's barracks, and had they had the sense to cut the telegraph line between Pagbilao and Lucena and the flimsy little "buzzer" line to Atimonan they eventually might have killed or captured the soldiers. An urgent telegram to Lucena for assistance brought Troop C over promptly.

A few days later the cavalry detachment was relieved and I with twenty men from Company E, 2nd Infantry, moved into Pagbilao. This temporary job was given to me, so I was told, because there were no junior infantry lieutenants in Lucena.

The cavalry soldier who took care of my horse and equipment, "striker" was the name the army gave it, and I rode the five miles, and I found myself the commanding officer of a town of some six thousand inhabitants built at the very foot of the high range of mountains that form the backbone of the island of Luzon. Between Pagbilao and Atimonan (on the Pacific Ocean) these steep jungle and tree-clad mountains are crowded into the seven mile isthmus that separates the China Sea from the Pacific Ocean. The mountains run in a series of ranges, separated by river-filled narrow valleys. At some time during the three hundred years of Spanish occupancy there was a wagon road between Pagbilao and Atimonan, but in June, 1901, no one would have believed it. The tropical rains had completely destroyed it; only in some sheltered spot could be seen the remains of a paved road. The buzzer line (this was a line of wire with a circumference of a piece of shoe thread) laid down by our splendid Signal Corps detachments followed a terrible trail up and down over the mountain ranges. Never have I seen a worse or more exhausting mountain trail.

The day following my enthronement in Pagbilao the village priest and the presidente invited me to lead the parade that evening in celebration of some local commemoration. There were two reasons why I didn't want to accept. The first reason was a military one. I had a vision of the insurgents stepping out of a side street and capturing me as I paraded around town, and the other was a feeling that a tall, thin, khaki clad lieutenant marching around town with a little tan colored presidente at his side, followed by a barefoot band, which, in turn, would be followed by a mass of Filipino men and women in their gala clothes, would look awfully silly.

After demurring for a time I accepted just to show the town I wasn't afraid of the guerrillas, and I left my revolver off too—that was a bit of swagger that I now think was foolish.

We had a grand parade, followed by a *baile*. I was installed in a large rocking chair and fed warm bottled beer while the youth of the town danced. Being not much over twenty-five years old myself, the dignity of the situation was too much for me. I went home at the first opportunity.

A few days later, realizing that the commanding officer's duties were nominal, that the position was a lonely one, and instead of waiting for the insurgents to attack me it might be a good idea to go out looking for them, I took ten infantrymen, one of our wagon mules, a big sixteen hand gray mule to pack food and cooking utensils for us, and started forth to carry the war to the enemy if they could be found. Not having a regulation pack saddle we used a native cross-buck saddle, lashing to it our few cooking utensils and rations.

Fearing that the commanding officer at Lucena might not approve of this expedition I arranged that the report of our departure not be sent until too late to recall us.

With a Filipino guide we started into the mountains early in the morning. The buzzer wire trail would climb straight up for several hundred feet, then descend at the same angle, cross a mountain stream and immediately go up again. This went on for mile after mile.

Some thirty-six hours later we arrived in Atimonan after the most strenuous foot journey I have ever taken. Although no insurgents were seen, we found the buzzer line cut where it crossed a little valley meadow, and I felt sure it was bait for an ambush. If it was, it didn't materialize as only two of us fixed it while the rest of the command kept under cover prepared for trouble.

Our big clumsy mule fell, head over heels, down several hundred feet of mountain, strewing our pots and pans and rations over the whole distance. With a cool mountain breeze blowing on our sweat soaked shirts, we slept that night in single file along the narrow trail, the men taking turns on guard until daybreak. That afternoon we marched into Atimonan where I found another company of the 2nd Infantry.

Atimonan was a small village built at the mouth of the Atimonan River and the southern end of Lamon Bay. The infantry took care of us that night, and the next morning we started off for Laguimanoc (leg of a chicken, the soldiers called it, because *manoc* is chicken in Tagalog) on Tayabas Bay.Laguimanoc is now called Padre Burgos.

Again the trail led us up and down through those terrible mountains. At one point a party of insurgents apparently attempted to ambush us, but they were discovered and we had a running fight down the side of a steep ravine before they got away. The natives had at least one casualty; we suffered no loss except a tremendous loss of energy in getting back out of that jungle-clad ravine. By map, our objective was barely ten miles from Atimonan—actually, including going astray for a mile or more, we traveled well over fifteen miles.

About dark reached Laguimanoc. Second Lieutenant J. C. Minus (W.P. 1899), 2nd Infantry, was in command at the time. My detachment was cared for by his company, and he gave me a room in his house. Laguimanoc being what it was, it is no reflection on my host's hospitality when I say that during the night it rained hard and I spent all of that period moving the bed around the room trying to escape the many little waterfalls from the mat ceiling.

There were two possible ways of returning to Pagbilao, by land through the mountains, or by sailing some twelve miles past the Pagbilao Grande Island in the Bay of Tayabas to Pagbilao. Having had my fill of tropical mountain climbing for a while, I decided to get a sailboat that could carry our mule, the ten soldiers and myself. The only thing we could find was a dugout canoe about thirty feet long with a big bamboo outrigger on the starboard side, a stout mast and sail. Although there were grave doubts as to the strength of the block and tackle on the canoe, we took the mule out on the little dock, cinched up the pack saddle, fastened the halyards to the saddle and hoisted our mule on board. He was put in the very center of the craft, his head tied to both gunwales, and although the sides of the canoe weren't much over three feet high and the beam where the mule stood was barely four feet, we made the trip in three or four hours without trouble. Of course that was due to the seamanship of the native captain and crew.

We sailed up Pagbilao Bay and a little river to the town. There was no dock and the water was too shallow to get the boat on the bank, and as it was impossible to persuade our worthy four-legged friend to jump overboard we manned the outrigger, raised it and dumped him into about three feet of water.

So ended the expedition. I can't say we accomplished anything of military value, save added knowledge of the country, and for me a lot of experience; but the guerrilla bands never attacked Pagbilao again.

This chapter on the Philippine Insurrection with its small battles and strenuous expeditions, interrupted by laughable if, for Babcock, not so laughable experiences, marked the passage of months and then years (1899-1902), of training of West Point graduates in the Regular service. It is worth setting out because this is what, apart from training at West Point, lay behind the abilities of Regular officers of the New Army in 1918. No wonder so many officers and men of the National Guard, and officers from the training schools and draft men of the

National Army, so-called, disliked, even hated, the sometimes pretensions of the Regulars, for the Regulars had little training, only applications of common sense; their training also was a set of experiences that had no application in Europe.

Is it worthwhile to show what the Old Army was like, if nothing else how it fostered an esprit when combined with the pride of being graduates of the U.S. Military Academy at West Point? One might advise a reader to skip the next two chapters and turn to the development of the New Army, taking the present chapter as sufficient for understanding the esprit. That may suffice for fast readers but it will not show the development of Babcock's judgment. Combined with his willingness to do duties differently, and change them if advisable, this preserved him from error when the New Army came into view beginning with the Battle of Soissons and then the crucial Battle of the Meuse-Argonne.

Three

Assignments

The first two chapters of Babcock's memoir are clear in their themes, the initial chapter covering the arrival at Manila and Iloilo, the second the Insurrection. The third is reminiscence of Troop F of the 1st Cavalry —the third its tradition of notable actions and commanders.

The opening of the third chapter might seem more detail than anyone, save a member of Troop F would appreciate. The present editor admits that when a close friend undertook to read the entire manuscript, and persevered, the volunteer reader lost attention in the few pages of the opening of this chapter. My advice to other readers is that this is all right, for the Old Army could be boring. The rest of the chapter is anecdotal but hardly boring. It tells of Fort Clark, Brackettville, Uvalde, Cline Station and Cline himself, San Francisco in 1906. Second Lieutenant Jerome Napoleon Bonaparte, maneuvers with the National Guard, Henri the drummer boy and soldier of fortune. Along the way five troops of the 7th Cavalry fought thousands upon thousands of Sioux warriors and lost at the Little Big Horn; one of Babcock's colonels had been a second lieutenant in the 2st Cavalry in 1876 and one of the first to see the battlefield where the 7th lost.

Special Order No. 181 War Department, August 3, 1904, was received and therein Conrad S. Babcock, first lieutenant, 3rd Cavalry, was promoted captain to rank from July 28, 1904, and assigned to the 1st Cavalry, Troop F.

In 1904 promotion orders of this nature were standard. If one compares this War Department order with the promotion order of a first lieutenant of today, the essential difference between line duty of the Old Army and the army of recent years becomes apparent. In this difference can be found the vital spark of interest so evident in the troop, regimental and branch morale of those days compared to today.

Note that by War Department order I was promoted to captain, 1st Cavalry, not captain of cavalry as today. There were fifteen captains in each regiment, one for each of twelve troops, three as regimental staff officers. Officers holding cavalry commissions were not just units in a huge pool of army officers as today; each of us belonged to a definite regiment and by War Department order was assigned to a definite troop. My captain's commission reads, "Captain, 1st Cavalry." My troop was F Troop in that regiment unless the regimental commander appointed me a staff officer. My status was fixed. Regardless of where I was, F Troop of the 1st Cavalry was my military family, I belonged to them. Because there was a 1st Cavalry and a Troop F was why I was a captain.

Troop F, which I had been commanding for nine months, had and still has a long, distinguished history. It was organized in May, 1834, at Camp Jackson, Arkansas Territory, as Company F, United States Regiment of Dragoons, Colonel Henry Dodge (ex-major of the Mounted Rangers), later to be the first governor of the Territory of Wisconsin, commanding. The company consisted of four sergeants, four corporals, and fifty men. Scarcely had this new organization entered upon their duties when the regiment left on an expedition against the Pawnee Indians. As the company officers had not yet reported, First Lieutenant Jefferson Davis (W.P. 1828), the regimental adjutant and twenty-seven years later the president of the Southern Confederacy, commanded Company F.

From 1834 to 1846, Company F served at numerous frontier stations in what, many years later, became the territories of Kansas, Arkansas and the Indian Territory, but at this time was just a vast, wild, almost unknown wilderness ruled by many Indian tribes. When the army of those days was not out in the field after Indians or escorting traders over the Santa Fe Trail to the independent Republic of Texas, it was hard at work constructing their log cabin garrisons, building rough furniture and raising vegetables. The Republic of Texas consisted of what is now Texas, the eastern half of what is now New Mexico, also southwestern Kansas and eastern Colorado. In May, 1836, Congress authorized another regiment of dragoons and the U.S. Dragoons became the 1st U.S. Regiment of Dragoons.

In 1846 the 1st Dragoons were sent to Matamoras (now opposite Fort Brown, Texas), which General Zachary Taylor had captured in May. In March, 1847, Company F went to Vera Cruz in General Winfield Scott's expedition and from there to the City of Mexico. After the war, in 1848, they were at Jefferson Barracks, Missouri. From this time to 1861 they were again on western frontier service in Missouri, Kansas, New Mexico, Colorado, and California constantly engaged in Indian expeditions.

In August, 1861, the title dragoons was changed to cavalry. In November, 1861, Company F, 1st Cavalry, with seven of the nine other companies sailed out of the Golden Gate, California, en route to Washington, D.C., via the Isthmus of Panama. After crossing the isthmus they re-embarked for New York on the steamship *North Star*. By December, 26, 1861, they were at Camp Sprague near Washington.

The story of the 1st Cavalry, until 1865, is the history of eighty-one battles, raids or skirmishes. They cover nearly all the battles fought by the Army of the Potomac under Generals McClellan, Pope, Hooker, Burnside, Meade and Grant. Of General Sheridan's Shenandoah campaign and his cavalry raids. After General Lee surrendered, the 1st Cavalry escorted General Sheridan to Petersburg and then returned to Washington. From there they went by rail to Cincinnati, Ohio, and by a Mississippi River steamer, the *Nicholas Longworth*, to New Orleans.

After Christmas, 1865, the regiment embarked for San Francisco via the Isthmus of Panama, and in January, 1866, was at the Presidio of San Francisco. Here the regiment was again divided, F Company going to Fort Union near Sacramento, California, and later to Oregon.

From 1866 to 1895, F Company served in California, Oregon, Washington, Idaho, Montana and Arizona, and as before the Civil War it spent much of its time marching after or fighting the Pi Utes, Bannock, Sioux and Apache Indians. In October, 1881, the title company was changed to troop.

In 1895, F Troop went to Fort Riley, Kansas, remaining there until April 19, 1898, when the regiment was again concentrated, after thirty-two years separation, at Camp George H. Thomas, Chickamauga Park, Georgia, in anticipation of war with Spain. A month later the regiment went to Lakeland, Florida, near Tampa. Troop F belonged to the squadron left behind when the regiment sailed for Cuba. In August the troop went to Camp Wickoff, Long Island, and to Fort Keogh, Montana, in October.

In August, 1901, it went to Fort Yellowstone, Montana, for a year. It then left for San Francisco where it embarked for the Philippines, sailing through the Golden Gate for the third time. After a year on the islands of Panay and Guimaras, it sailed for home and in October, 1903, was stationed at Fort Clark, Texas.

The history of Fort Clark begins on the twentieth of June, 1852, when two companies, C and E, of the 1st Infantry, under command of Captain Joseph H. LaMotte (W.P. 1827), occupied the land about the Las Moras spring for a camp as a guard for the San Antonio and Eagle Pass wagon road and for the protection of the Rio Grande border against depredations by Mexicans and Indians. The camp was first called Fort Riley as a compliment to Colonel Bennet Riley (1813) of the 1st Infantry, but at that officer's suggestion the name was changed to Fort Clark by orders dated July 15, 1852, in honor of Major John B. Clark (W.P. 1813), 1st Infantry, who died during the Mexican War.

A few days after the camp was named, a lease was entered into for the use of the site for military purposes between the owner, Samuel Maverick, and Lieutenant Colonel D. D. Tompkins (W.P. 1820) of the quartermaster's department, on the part of the United States, for a period not to exceed twenty years, at the rate of fifty dollars per month.

In March, 1861, the garrison of five companies left the fort in compliance with orders from General David E. Twiggs, the commanding general, department of Texas. This order was issued on March 8, 1861, but the records show that General Twiggs, a southern sympathizer, had been dismissed from the Federal Army on March 1, 1861. The orders from Washington probably didn't arrive for weeks after their promulgation. Twiggs became a major general in the Confederate Army.

After the Federal infantry abandoned the fort, three companies of Texas Confederate infantry occupied it for a short time, but as the garrison was far from the scene of hostilities Clark was again abandoned until 1866, when U.S. Regulars reoccupied it, and in spite of many recommendations including that of the officer commanding the army, Lieutenant General William T. Sherman (W.P. 1840), that Fort Clark be abandoned, it is still a Texas border station for the army. Bracketville, a little town with a population probably more than half Mexican, was just east of the post. It had a shop or two, a little hotel, several saloons, two of them were known as "The Blue Goose" and "The Bucket of Blood." Between the post and town was a magnificent spring, the waters from which ran in a fine clear stream halfway around the garrison buildings, eventually, I suppose, finding its way through the flat cactus and mesquite prairie to the Rio Grande, some fifty miles south.

Fort Clark was in Kinney County about 145 miles west of San Antonio and ten miles north of the Southern Pacific Railroad.

The officers' quarters and barracks were built of stone. The stables were long sheds without side walls, the feed mangers running down the center. China berry trees struggled for existence in their beds dug in the "colechi" subsoil upon which the post was built. This was another garrison still in the Standard Oil wick trimming era, but we did have a fairly modern bathroom. The toilet being a shed in the yard.

Quail, both bob-white and blue, were plentiful. In the autumn duck shooting was excellent and near at hand, and twelve or fifteen miles away in the mountains one could find deer and occasionally wild turkeys. The summer months were terrible, but most of the year the climate was delightful. Even then, however, when a Texas norther hit us the cool bracing temperatures of an ideal day would drop in a few minutes to freezing.

2

From September, 1904, to February, 1908, marks one of the most enjoyable, happiest and beneficial periods of my army service. I reported for duty to Colonel Martin B. Hughes, 1st Cavalry (W.P. 1869), on September 30, and after a separation of three years again became a proud member of the fine old 1st Cavalry.

Colonel Hughes was a unique character. He had a sharp tongue, a complete command of verbal reprimand, and he could instantly spot a toady. Anyone endeavoring to soft soap the colonel went out of his office with confusion at the old man's sarcasm. What happened in his office was not carried out of the building; he could "crawl" an offender unmercifully and shortly afterwards shake him for the drinks at the nearby club.

Colonel Hughes left the regiment in 1906, his place being taken by Lieutenant Colonel Edward J. McClernand (W.P. 1870). In June, 1876, Colonel McClernand, then a second lieutenant, was a member of Brigadier General A. H. Terry's command that moved against the Sioux Indians under Gall, Crazy Horse, Rain-in-the-face, and their medicine man, Sitting Bull. This was the expedition in which the 7th Cavalry under Lieutenant Colonel George A. Custer (W.P. 1861) was defeated, Brevet Major General Custer and all the members of five troops of his regiment being killed. McClernand was one of the first members of General Terry's command to see the battlefield after the engagement. Colonel McClernand was the holder of a Medal of Honor for "Most distinguished gallantry in action against hostile Nez Perce Indians at Bear Paw Mountain, Montana, on September 30, 1877." What an opportunity I had to learn interesting sidelights on these fights but I never did so; young officers, as a rule, are uninterested in the experiences of their elders.

In March, 1906, I marched the regimental band to Fort Sam Houston where it participated in the annual flower carnival in commemoration of the defense of the Alamo in February, 1836. The band instruments were carried in a light wagon; the twenty-eight members of the band rode their horses, which were old and selected for the band more because of their dispositions than for soundness or marching ability. We marched to Fort Sam Houston in six days, camping at Cline, Uvalde, Sabinal, Hondo, and Castroville—a distance of about 140 miles.

At the end of the second day's march we rode up the main street of Uvalde, better known now than then, since its leading citizen, John N. Garner, became the vice president of the United States. As we rode up the dusty street past the town's best hotel (a two-story little wooden affair) a cavalry officer recently retired hailed. Later he invited me up to his little hot bedroom, took out a bottle of beer from a barrel, and proceeded to tell me how he intended augmenting his retired pay by operating a chicken ranch and selling the product to both Fort Sam Houston and Fort Clark. Then we went out of town and he showed me his egg factory. It was a pathetic sight. In a field well covered with mesquite trees he had cleared out an area about one hundred feet long by fifty feet wide. Hereon he had built a huge cage, top, sides and ends of chicken wire. Inside two or three large mesquite trees had been left, and on and under this protection from rain, snow or blazing sun roamed several dozen chickens. No special types of layers predominated, just any old hen that he had been able to purchase from farmers in the vicinity. His chicken ranch failure wasn't prolonged. Not long after my visit I heard he had left Uvalde.

On April 18, 1906, word came of the San Francisco earthquake and fire. A day or two later we started our return march and when two days out of Fort Sam Houston, Colonel Hughes telegraphed us that the regiment was under orders to go to San Francisco and for me to expedite my return. We were about ninety miles from Fort Clark. By marching forty-five miles a day we rode into the garrison early in the afternoon of the second day. To show how good they were, the band the next morning went to guard mount on their horses. Four days from Fort Sam Houston to Fort Clark. Of course, the band did not carry rifles, but on band horses it was quite a performance. I have never heard of any organization equaling that time between these army posts. The noncommissioned officers of the 1s t Cavalry band laughed at troop friends who attempted to tell them how to march cavalry.

In several trains the entire regiment was moved to San Francisco. Each squadron with all their tentage, wagons, horses, mules and baggage went in a single train. By this method, as a squadron of four large troops arrived at Third and Townsend Street Station of the Southern Pacific Railroad, they detrained, packed their wagons, saddled up and marched out to the presidio.

Regimental headquarters, the band, and eight troops encamped in the presidio. One squadron went to Oakland. The train carrying regimental headquarters reached San Francisco first, and Colonel Hughes directed me to ride out to the presidio and find out where we were to camp. Riding west on Third Street, I passed through a completely fire swept section of the city. It was fire that almost destroyed San Francisco. The earthquake shook the city about 5:18 a.m., and a short time later when each household began the preparation of breakfast, houses started to catch fire in many parts of the city, due to cracked chimneys and fire flues.

Riding my horse through this all but deserted city, the streets strewn with bricks, stones and charred timbers, I had a stupendous example of what an uncontrolled conflagration can do to a big American city built of wood. Cooking inside any house had been forbidden. In front of all unburned and occupied houses west of Van Nest Avenue cook stoves had been erected, either on the sidewalks or on the front lawns. It was an odd sight to see numbers of dinners being prepared, al fresco, for block after block. As I led my horse down Pierce Street from Pacific Avenue to Union a nice looking woman who was leaning over her cook stove looked up at me and said, "Soldier, would you like a carrot for your horse?" I, as one representative of a thousand cavalrymen who had come hundreds of miles to give protection and assistance to the inhabitants of an almost completely wrecked city, suddenly found myself being offered something by the first person who had spoken to me. Certainly the spirit of old San Francisco had not been consumed; we soon had this impression confirmed daily.

For more than a month the regiment patrolled the city streets, took charge of tent camps in Golden Gate Park, and did everything possible to assist the homeless. In the meantime dozens of lost dogs—mutts and princes—attached themselves to a dog's best friend, the enlisted man of our army; our camp was soon full of them. Many men became so attached to their refugee dogs that they took them back to Texas; but the heat of July Texas was too much for some of these well bred California acclimated dogs, in a short time most of them seemed to have disappeared.

In compliance with an order of Brigadier General Funston, then commanding the department of California, I was appointed a surveying officer to act upon the loss of public property destroyed by the recent earthquake and fire in the city of San Francisco and vicinity, "in such cases as may be referred to him." My surveying consisted in riding my horse downtown to some street where I would find a mass of burned wood, fallen bricks or stones, and be told that therein had been stored so many thousands of dollars of medical, quartermaster, or such like property. I have no doubt these statements were true, but I couldn't help thinking what a blessing some of these fires might have been to some of the accountable officers.

Sometime in May we were back in Texas. Drills, target practice and the general routine life of a cavalry garrison engaging our attention as the hot Texas summer took over Kinney County.

The passenger and freight station for Fort Clark and Bracketville was Spofford on the Southern Pacific Railroad. The next station east was Cline, named after an ex-soldier of the Mounted Rifles, now called the 3rd Cavalry, who was the station agent during my service at Fort Clark. Whenever a cavalry command marched through or stopped at Station Cline for lunch or the night, old Cline would call on the commanding officer with a big drinking glass, a bottle of whiskey, and some liquid honey. He would then pour out a generous three-fingered drink, add a spoonful of honey—the army was expected to furnish the water—and for the honor of the cavalry, past and present, one had to down the old mounted rifleman's slug.

During part of Cline's service in the cavalry he served under Second Lieutenant Jerome Napoleon Bonaparte (W.P. 1852), Mounted Rifles. Lieutenant Bonaparte was the grandson of Napoleon I's brother, Jerome Bonaparte, who married Miss Elizabeth Patterson of Baltimore in 1803, later had that marriage annulled and married Princess Catherine of Wuertemburg and became King of Westphalia in 1807.

Cline told me this story about Bonaparte, who does not appear to have been very popular with his command. Lieutenant Bonaparte's cavalry company had been marching in the rain all day, and after supper in camp, the rain having stopped, the men were sitting around a big log fire drying themselves and their rifle ammunition. In those days the cavalryman carried a 58-caliber muzzle loading rifled gun, fired by a hammer falling on a percussion cap. The ammunition was carried in pouches and consisted of paper cartridges loaded with the round lead ball in the bottom and the powder on top. To load, the rifleman bit or tore off the closed end of the cartridge with his teeth and poured the powder down the barrel from the muzzle, then rammed in a wad of paper, then poured in the bullet and rammed down another wad. If the cartridges got wet, the men used to dry them out in the sun or as they were doing as described by Cline.

Bonaparte's little canvas tent was not far from the fire, and in order to start a fire in his sheet iron stove (probably what we used to call a Sibley tent stove) he walked out to the fire and with his little stove shovel took up a shovel load of wood coals and, unknown to him, a number of rifle cartridges. No one warned him. He returned to his tent while the cavalrymen sat quiet expectantly eyeing the lieutenant's tent. In a few seconds there was a violent explosion, the stove tore itself loose from the chimney, the tent caught fire and before the conflagration had been put out, poor Mr. Bonaparte had little more than half a tent in which to spend the night.

Cline was in Texas when the secretary of war, Mr. Jefferson Davis, conceived the idea of using camels to carry the mail through the desert region between San Antonio and, I believe, El Paso. This was some time between 1853–1857; but the attempt was unsuccessful. Cline said that for many years after the mail project had been given up, camels that had escaped or been turned loose were occasionally seen running wild in south Texas.

3

In his reminiscences of the 1st Cavalry, Babcock like all other members of the Old Army in the 1890s and turn of the twentieth century, at least down to the appearance of the New Army in 1918, could not help taking a shot or two at the National Guard. The Guard came into existence at this time and these were the summer soldiers, their officers likely as green as the men themselves. The organization of the Guard was a slow process, but in fact not as slow as Babcock thought, for in 1918 the Guard divisions showed themselves as good, even better, than the so-called Regular divisions. The latter were themselves composed of draft men, not Old Army men. Even the First Division, which went over to France in the summer of 1917, in a confused order and understaffed, was not an Old Army division—there was none in 1917–18.

Having disposed of the National Guard to his satisfaction, and his criticism of joint maneuvers then and later contained much good sense. Babcock turned to the story of Henri the drummer boy.

One summer, we marched to Mabry, Texas, near Austin. Here the entire regiment with other Regular Army and National Guard organizations had "maneuvers." The march up and back was good field training, but the maneuvers were as impracticable as have been all such exercises that I have seen. Of course, the National Guard soldier at maneuvers is really spending his hard earned vacation from his livelihood job, and he is apt to look at the training camp period as a picnic. Who can blame him? When one of the National Guard regiments left camp by train they waved at us, out of a car window, several troop guidons that had disappeared a few nights before from in front of the troop commanders' tents.

One military exercise consisted of the employment of cavalry to reconnoiter an assumed entrenched position held by, as I now remember, a brigade of infantry The cavalry—fifteen troops of the 1st and 5th Cavalry under Lieutenant Colonel Charles H. Watts (W.P. 1872) – left camp early in the morning. Then the "enemy" infantry took up their battle positions north of camp. When three or four miles out of camp, Colonel Watts halted his command, assembled all the squadron and troop commanders, and on a small scale map proceeded to allot to each troop for reconnaissance certain sections of the battle front. I am convinced the colonel hadn't the least idea how to accomplish his mission. He would call up a troop commander, point to the little map and with a finger rub it over an indefinite area covering several square miles and then tell him to move out and find the enemy. Nothing was said about reports or where to send any information gained. Well, in a few moments he had most if not all his command scattered over a large area consisting of low, well wooded hills, many ravines and few roads.

As the last troop of my regiment prepared to leave, I realized that as the commanding officer of the 1st Cavalry, Colonel McClernand, was not present that day, had no command and wasn't expected to do anything by Watts. So in order to at least get a bit of amusement out of the affair I got permission to go off on a scout with my orderly and a bugler. Following a trail through some woods we discovered a platoon of the enemy National Guard cavalry picketing the trail crossing of a narrow ravine. Spreading out my two man command over a front of about one hundred yards under close cover, we dismounted and crawled up to our edge of the ravine. At a signal we began firing our pistols, the bugler furiously blew the "Charge," I shouted commands for such and such troops to surround the enemy from both flanks, we cheered and howled and in less than a minute the enemy dashed for their horses, mounted and fled in wild confusion. It was a magnificent victory; so after we were able to stop laughing we mounted and followed our frightened enemy.

Just at this moment Captain William G. Sills (W.P. 1895), 1st Cavalry, and his bugler rode up. He had been commanding a squadron, but after Watts got through with it Sills decided there was nothing for him to do and rode off (as I had done) to see what the "war" was about. Sills and I were great friends; both of us played polo and often went shooting together. Now with two captains, two buglers and a private, our powerful force proceeded down a narrow road towards the enemy's lines. Five or ten minutes later we sighted the advance guard of a battalion of, as I now remember, Arkansas infantry. Moving off the road into thick cover we let the advance guard go past, then rode out in front of the major commanding the enemy battalion and told him he was surrounded by cavalry. He said that no blank ammunition had been issued to his command; he couldn't even shoot, and was glad to surrender anyhow.

From there we skirted the left flank of the enemy's main line and found ourselves in rear of a Regular Army infantry company. Realizing that our campaign was about over, we decided to die in a blaze of glory. So, again, we simulated a large force, both buglers blew the "Charge" and the bugle call for "Commence Firing," both captains and the private fired their pistols and uttered loud and wild shouts and orders. For a moment or two there was a bit of confusion in the enemy's line, but when an umpire rode up and made us tell the strength of our force, he laughed and said it was certainly a gallant attempt but he must rule us out of action.

Maneuvers of large forces are a pure waste of time unless the senior commanders know their jobs and the squads, platoons and troops or companies have been thoroughly trained in basic field tactics. In my opinion maneuvers or the combined employment and simulated fighting tactics of all branches of the service should be drilled, not just left open to all manner of absurd tactical situations. Once the bullet is withdrawn from the copper shell there is no possible way to restore to blank cartridge combat the sense of personal danger, the fear of capture and the destruction of the men under one's command. These are the elements that decide battles. In defensive and offensive maneuver situations there are usually several possible solutions; but always there is one tactical operation that seems to give the best chance of success. A man with an active tactical imagination will see that chance at once.

Having decided on the operation, all officers and men engaged should be informed as to the main features of the combined operations and, in detail, as to what is expected of their own particular unit. Then the troops should execute their orders, great stress being laid on individual initiative, especially in small units executing military evolutions. If any part of the combined operation is incorrectly executed the maneuver should be stopped, troops withdrawn and the whole operation repeated. Of course, before anything of this nature is attempted, the troops must be fully equipped, the individual officers and enlisted men thoroughly trained in the tactics of their arm, and the regimental, brigade, division, corps, and army commanders be officers who have had, if possible, actual battle experience or at least are capable of judging the operation of small units in motion. Battles are won by courageous, well trained small units. Maneuvers are won by courageous, well trained small units. Maneuvers such as were held in the summer of 1940 in several of our army areas were more absurd than usual, unequipped, untrained troops, and commanded by generals who had never commanded or seen troops in modern war.

Babcock referred to 1940, but it was the 1941 summer maneuvers in Louisiana that attracted national attention. Their "mock" nature was clear enough, as the opposing forces that summer did not have enough equipment and it was necessary to label trucks as "tanks."

Before concluding this brief account of the happy, simple life of the grand old 1st Cavalry in Fort Clark, Texas, I must record the story of a soldier of fortune I met one day in our post library. He was of average height, sun-browned complexion, dressed in a well worn blue uniform and the forage cap of the 1894 vintage. Often I had seen him collecting things off the post dump. I thought he was a Mexican inhabitant of Bracketville. As I entered the library he bowed and said in perfectly pronounced English, "Our library is greatly depleted, captain." His remark was correct, as the librarian had been throwing away many worn out books, but the use of the word "depleted" from a Mexican scavenger aroused my interest, and we began to talk. This is a synopsis of his tale.

In 1863 the French Army under Marshal Bazaine was engaged in conquering Mexico for the Archduke Maximilian who landed at Vera Cruz in 1864. One of the very youthful drummer boys in this army was my library friend, and because I have forgotten his name I will call Henri. When Napoleon III under strong diplomatic pressure from President Lincoln backed up by the presence of a large army on the United States-Mexican border under Major General Sheridan withdrew his support of the Austrian archduke, then Emperor of Mexico, the French Army left the country. In some unexplained way, drummer boy Henri was left behind in the City of Mexico. Immediately the Mexican Army of President Benito Juarez drafted him in a regiment stationed on the west coast of Mexico far below the U.S. border. Unable to desert, Soldado Enrico served in the Mexican Army for five years along that coast.

Finally, he was transferred to a regiment stationed on the Mexican-U.S. border; from this point he immediately deserted to the United States. Wandering along the border he encountered a troop of our 8th Cavalry and enlisted in our army. This seems to have been about 1873. For thirty years Henry served in our army, finally being retired as a first sergeant in the 9th Infantry, I believe. He saw service against the Indians in the 1870s and 1880s, the Spanish-American War and the Philippine Insurrection.

At the end of each enlistment period he sought out some South American war or governmental disturbance and spent the months of his U.S. Army reenlistment furlough as a volunteer on the side that offered him the highest rank. As I now remember his story, he had been a major in Venezuela, a captain in Nicaragua, besides other commissioned grades in different wars and rebellions.

"And now," he said to me, "I have come back to Bracketville because once I served here at Fort Clark. I have a little shack, and I engaged an old Mexican woman to cook and care for the house. As you know, the town has recently had a religious revival, and the minister came to me and said, 'Sergeant, either you marry this woman or leave town.' All I have in the world is this little house. I cannot sell it" and so, "Captain," he said with a typical French shrug and futile wave of the hands, "I marry her."

Four

More of the Same

In November, 1907, the regiment less three troops left by rail for San Francisco and the Philippine Islands. At Fort Sam Houston one troop (H) and at Fort Clark two troops (D and I) remained to care for all the horses left behind for the 3rd Cavalry which was coming from the Philippines. Caring for some five hundred animals at Fort Clark, in addition to the usual care and protection of the garrison property, was no small job. While the two troops took the usual care of their own mounts, all that could be done with the other animals was to feed, water and doctor them and let them exercise in the stable yards.

Colonel McClernand permitted me to remain at Fort Clark in command. On November 14, 1907, my son Charles Parmelee was born in San Francisco, and in January, 1908, I left Fort Clark, on leave, ahead of the three troops, due to sail from San Francisco in March, 1908, on the United States Army transport *Sherman*.

Babcock married Marion Eells in San Francisco in 1902 and a first son, Stanton, was born a year later.

1

As the *Sherman* lay at anchor in the, to me, familiar Iloilo Strait opposite the town of Iloilo, island of Panay, Marion and I went ashore in a launch and drove out to Jaro, the site of my first insurrecto adventures.

Upon returning to Iloilo we found the launch had gone, and anxious not to miss the ship on which were our two small boys and a nurse we hired a native to sail us out to the transport. Boarding a craft very similar to the outrigger canoe I had once sailed off in with ten infantry soldiers and a mule, we started down the little river which served Iloilo as a ship's harbor. Coming up the stream was a small steam tug and, immediately, signals and shouts were exchanged between the crews. Knowing that, at least theoretically, a vessel under sail has the right of way over a steamer, I paid no attention to our skipper's navigation. As we drew near, however, it became evident that the tug's captain had not the slightest intention of altering his course, and apparently our captain couldn't or didn't know how to tack his craft out of the tug's way. Amidst yells and imprecations the tug steamed right over our starboard outrigger. The canoe heeled over wildly and for a moment or two I thought we were all going down. Finally we sailed out of the river into the strait where the tides run with great force and sped between the island of Panay and the little island of Guimaras.

The transport looked near at hand but our little shallow vessel tacked back and forth for what seemed an hour before we were able to make fast to a big lighter tied to the *Sherman* and upon which the property of the infantry going ashore for station on the island of Guimaras was being loaded.

The next day we were in Manila. From there we took the Manila-Dagupan Railroad to Camp Stotsenburg, named for the late Colonel John M. Stotsenburg (W.P. 1881), captain of cavalry commanding the 1st Nebraska Volunteer Infantry, killed in April, 1899, in a fight with Aguinaldo's command between Malolos and Quingua. Quingua is now called Flaridel, Bulacan Province.

At Camp Stotsenburg, Troops D, H, and I rejoined their squadrons; I took up my duties as regimental adjutant and we were soon comfortably settled with a Chinaman cook, an amah (nurse), a Filipino laundress, a Filipino houseboy and a Filipino stable boy and valet. Quite a numerous ménage in a house that really deserved only the title of pinewood shack. These shacks stood on stilts. A rough frame of two by four beams, covered on the outside by unpainted pine boards, between which daylight and starlight entered more easily each day as the tropical heat shrank the green timbers. The roof was of galvanized iron, the toilet the dry earth cans system. The shower bath a delicious cold stream piped from the nearby hills that fell on the split bamboo floor of the bath shed and then on the ground. The sides of the house were mostly wide windows with heavy wooden shutters that hung on hinges from the window top. The house proper consisted of a combination sitting and dining room, two bedrooms. In the boys' room I had part partitioned off for the amah. A porch ran around three sides of the house. Beyond the back porch was the kitchen, three servants' rooms, toilet and shower. Room partitions extended only part of the distance to the roof. One could sit in any room and follow the little bright colored lizards as they chased bugs or butterflies over the roof beams. The lizards were usually very sure footed, but occasionally in the wild excitement of a chase after some especially appetizing tropical night bug the little fellows would fall on the dining room table during our meals, so over the table we hung a huge Japanese paper umbrella. After that, when a misstep occurred the little reptiles would slither down the top of the umbrella, hit the floor running and in a moment be up aloft after game again. All the beds were covered with mosquito netting against that dreaded pest, the malarial mosquito.

The regiment wore made to measure English Hong Kong uniforms, light khaki colored pith helmets, and in bad weather the campaign cap. The officers had caps also, and on their helmets was sewn a khaki pugaree. The white starched cotton coat with high collar was not changed to the much cooler and more comfortable low turned down coat collar until thirty years later. The hot sun of the tropics has been beating down on the heads of the American officers and soldiers for over forty years. Why in all those years someone in authority has not made it impossible to put the army under the campaign hat in the Philippines, Panama, and in the Hawaiian Islands, I have never understood.

Even while the 1st Cavalry was wearing the helmet on foot or mounted, I have heard officers say that one couldn't ride in it, it bobbed off the head. This was sheer nonsense; we even wore it during polo games. It was wonderfully cool, the sweatband being offset from the body of the helmet by small thin round pieces of cork. This allowed the air to blow over one's head. Unless you have worn the felt campaign hat in the hot sun of the tropics you can't begin to appreciate the relief the helmet gives. In the department of Panama in 1932, the department commander, Major

General Preston Brown, required the command to wear steel helmets at department reviews, but neither he nor any of his staff wore them.

At Fort Clark shortly after being appointed regimental adjutant I wrote to the quartermaster general of the army and asked for one of the original United States dragoons blouse buttons that I knew the Q.M. department had stored away. This request was complied with, and from this button we had solid gold plated buttons made, exact models of the original button, except that under the spread eagle the date 1833 was added. The button was ¾ inches in diameter, oval in shape; the spread eagle has on his breast a shield with the letter D superimposed thereon. There is an olive branch in the eagle's right claw and three arrows in the left claw. With the approval of Colonel McClernand the officers wore this button screwed into the front of the campaign hat.

Since the Great War (I) all Regular Army regiments wear special regimental insignia, but in 1906, I think the old dragoon button worn by the 1st Cavalry was the first insignia worn by any regiment of our army. When the 1st Cavalry discontinued wearing the dragoon button I do not know—sometime after the war perhaps, when all those who knew the fine history of the regiment had left it.

At formal social evening affairs the officers wore white mess jackets, formal dress shirts and collars, black tie, white braid rank insignia on the sleeves, buff cuffs (part of the colors of the U.S. dragoons), two rows of three brass buttons each on the front of the jacket, and a white full dress waistcoat closed with three small brass buttons. For ordinary evening wear we wore the high collared white uniform, braided around the collar, down the front and around the bottom of the coat. With both the mess jacket and the white blouse, white trousers and white shoes were worn and the white cap.

We invited the 10th Cavalry polo team, then at Fort McKinley near Manila, to visit us. This they did and we were defeated in every game, but each defeat was a good lesson. The governor general of the P.I., W. Cameron Forbes, brought his team up too and we raised our morale by beating them. As captain of the polo team I received authority from the division commander to take the team to Jolo, island of Jolo, to play the 6th Cavalry. That was a grand trip. We took about twenty ponies and the following officers: Captains William G. Sills, Robert C. Foy, Herbert H.

Brees, First Lieutenants Clarence Lininger, Frank Keller, Second Lieutenant J. Mayhew Wainwright and myself.

In the above unconscious recital of buttons, helmets, waistcoats, etc., the subject naturally turned to polo. All this from an officer as intelligent as Conrad Babcock. He wrote his account in 1940–41 before the name of General Douglas MacArthur's replacement in the besieged Philippine Islands, the then Lieutenant General Wainwright, doomed to capture and three and one-half years of imprisonment by the Japanese Army, became known throughout the United States.

Jolo is in the Sulu archipelago and was famous as a deep sea pearl fishing area, also as one of the Malay inhabited islands still in more or less insurrection against the United States, but more than anything else it had the ill fame as the home of the natives who practiced juramentado.

The word stood for Filipinos who, in anticipation of a future life of bliss, suddenly chose to kill all infidels they met, usually with the bolo.

Rifle, carbine and revolver firing have been very thoroughly practiced in the Regular Army since my earliest remembrance. Each year, at the end of the regular target season, selected officers and enlisted men in each of the administrative divisions or departments into which the states were divided were assembled at some suitable garrison where a competition was held. Those making the team were given gold, silver, or bronze medals. After an officer or soldier had won three such medals he was carried on the rolls of the War Department as a distinguished marksman (or pistol shot) and awarded a gold medal.

At Fort Sill, Oklahoma, in August, 1906, I won a bronze medal at the southwestern division competition. In 1907 at Camp Theodore J. Wint, Leon Springs, Texas, I actually won the top (gold) medal, more because the competition happened not to be very severe than to any great improvement in my ability to shoot on the target range. That was shown when I failed to make the army team at Fort Sheridan, Illinois, a few weeks later. The officers who failed to make the army team were ordered to Camp Perry, Ohio, as range officers for the big national match. Range officers were called "sand rats" when one drew a job in the target butts under Lieutenant Colonel Robert K. Evans (W.P. 1875) and his assistants who ran the national individual and national pistol matches and the matches of the National Rifle Association. Here one could see the finest rifle and revolver shots in the United States, one might even say in the world. Certainly there is no country where there are any better rifle and revolver shots than in the U.S., and in my opinion there is no army or navy or marine corps in Europe or Asia that can compete successfully with our teams in small arms firing.

At Camp Perry, as I have said, one sees the great rifle and revolver experts, who are often the greatest cranks imaginable. As they approach the firing point they fire their rifles several times into pits specially built for that purpose. This is done, one is told, to slightly soil the barrel of the rifle the competitor has spent hours cleaning and oiling. Then they set up their high powered telescopes, open their record books, wherein they have recorded every shot they have fired since they graduated from air rifles. By watching the range flags and through the telescope the heat waves rising straight up or drifting across the face of the target, the expert sets his rifle rear sight with his micrometer. Then he fires his first preliminary shot. Unless the shot is a bull's eye or a twelve o'clock four (just under the bull's eye) the average rifle fanatic will return to his "dope" book, his telescope or field glasses, his micrometer. Of course, the reason I laugh at these experts is because I never had the patience to follow their methods, neither had I the temperament to let a rifle kick me all day long and not get a bit gun shy or nervous.

In May, 1909, the Philippine division rifle and pistol competition was held at Fort William McKinley and there I acquired my third competitive medal (a bronze one) and I was carried on the War Department rolls as a distinguished marksman. "Discretion being the better part of valor," I have never attended a competition since. Unless one wears medals or badges indicating former skill with firearms, displays horse show cups or recounts his equestrian exploits, the army soon forgets its shooting experts or trained horsemen. A somewhat annoying, yet quite natural, example of this occurred to me when I took command of the 1st Cavalry at Marfa, Texas, in 1926. I rode out to the target range to observe the firing of one of my troops. Just to recall old times and to see how I could handle the old Springfield rifle, the same model we had used since 1903, I decided to fire a few shots at five hundred yards. As I laid down at the firing point, adjusted the sling and prepared to fire, one of my fine young lieutenants knelt down beside me and began to give me some advice about the gun and how to shoot it. Although I shooed him away, it was evident that he was just trying to help "the old man," and that reputations made seventeen years before could not be known by a young officer who was hardly in the cap pistol age at that time.

The tropics do funny things to the Caucasian. One day, shortly after noon, I left the adjutant's office at Camp Stotsenburg for my quarters across the parade ground. When about halfway across I suddenly heard a shot apparently coming from the quarters of Troop F, 1st Cavalry. As other shots were heard, out from that barracks poured a stream of soldiers, running down the steps and jumping out of the windows. As they landed, they ran shouting in all directions or hid under the barracks. I turned and ran towards the barracks. I half suspected that someone's mental balance had slipped and that for some unknown reason he was firing a high-powered rifle or revolver in barracks. So, as I reached the sidewalk in front of the barracks, my suspicion was confirmed when a soldier with a rifle ran out the front door of the barracks and came rapidly down the steps towards me. He was holding the rifle diagonally across his body, about waist high, and he made me feel rather conspicuous.

In spite of shouts of warning by men under the barracks, it was certainly my duty as an officer to do something. So I walked towards the soldier. As he stopped and I anticipated he might fire at me, I raised my little cane (called a swagger stick) and said in a sharp commanding tone, "Drop that gun." Discipline worked. His wildness left him in a flash; he recognized one of his regimental officers and he dropped his rifle instantly. As that loaded gun crashed on the sidewalk, my morale rose rapidly.

He was Private Mike Beecham, Troop F, 1st Cavalry, who for some fancied wrongs had gone berserk. He killed the first sergeant of F Troop, William Hoey, also Privates Thomas J. Woodward, George Wilson, and Edward Clark, and wounded Privates Harry H. Whipple and Emmett Dampeer. He was tried by the court of first instance in Pampanga in 1909 and given life imprisonment by Judge Julie Lorente. He appealed the sentence, I believe, and on March 16, 1910, the supreme court of the Philipines changed the sentence to execution. The acting governor, Gilbert, commuted the sentence back to life imprisonment. He was released from Bilibid prison and deported to the United States on November 9, 1919. What has since become of this man I have never heard.

2

In August, 1911, I had been relieved from assignment to the 1st Cavalry, so now I was assigned to the 10th Cavalry, then stationed at Fort Ethan Allen, Vermont, and by regimental order was assigned to Troop C. From Fort Myer we traveled by train to Fort Ethan Allen. The maples, elms and oaks of New England were rapidly staining their leaves with the indescribable hues and tints that only cold, free nature can provide. Yes, we were back in Vermont, admiring the beautiful hillsides, keeping the home fires burning, and shaking naphthalene out of our winter underwear.

The 10th Cavalry was not destined to spend another winter in Vermont. In November the regiment was under orders to proceed to Arizona by ship and rail. Marion and Parmelee went to New York City to spend the time it would take the regiment to make the journey, joining me at Fort Huachuca. As it was reported there was no school for ten-year-old boys in our new garrison, and as Mr. and Mrs. Eells offered to care for Stanton in San Francisco and put him in school there, he went with his grandmother. This marked the first of the almost inevitable separations that mar the home life of the army family.

Going to New York City by rail we embarked on an army transport and a few days later disembarked at Galveston, Texas. Here and at nearby Texas City was the large force that had been assembled as an expeditionary force for the invasion of the Republic of Mexico should the administration decide to intervene in the revolution in that country, but being fought out generally along the U.S.—Mexican border.

Not many months before our arrival this Texas City force had gone through a devastating hurricane that all but washed away the entire camp, built on the low flat shores of Galveston Bay. One of my classmates, Captain G. Maury Crallé of the infantry, told me his regiment had thirteen miles of drainage ditches around their camp alone. We were standing near the shore of the bay; I noticed a small dark object moving slowly far out in the water, and was told it was a man going swimming. As he was still wading, it appeared he might almost walk out of sight of land before finding water deep enough to swim. No wonder the ocean at high tide and with a terrific wind behind it was able to drive far inland.

Again we entrained, and a few days later via the Southern Pacific Railroad to El Paso, Texas, and from there on over the El Paso and Southwestern Railroad we arrived one rather dismal day at Fort Huachuca, Arizona, relieving the 5th Cavalry under Colonel W. K. Wilder (W.P. 1877). The 10th Cavalry went into camp on the parade ground in front of the barracks they were to occupy as soon as the 5th Cavalry should vacate, but we found the officers' quarters, barracks and stables in bad shape and the post generally rundown. As the son of a very loyal 5th Cavalryman, it made me wonder what Colonel Wesley Merritt would have said, could he have been present when his famous old command turned over such a cavalry garrison to an incoming organization.

Fort Huachuca is situated on the northwestern side of the Huachuca Mountains in Cochise County at an altitude of 5,306 feet above sea level. It is about twenty miles north of the Sonora, Mexico, line and twenty-two miles southwest of Tombstone. The reservation covers about 44,800 acres. The post was established as a camp in 1877. In 1881, Major General Irvin McDowell (W.P. 1838) reported to the War Department that many of the Arizona Territory posts had been abandoned on account of sickness, that Huachuca had been found to be healthy and should be made a permanent post. We found the all-year-round climate unbeatable, never very cold, and never hot. Sunsets no artist would dare copy. Many times in the clear, pure, dry air I have seen the sun go down in a blaze of the solar spectrum, followed a few seconds later by a 360-degree gorgeous horizon, more brilliant in the east than in the west.

Back in the 1860s and 1870s when my father in the 5th Cavalry was stationed at the San Carlos Indian Reservation or out after Apaches, and even as late as the early 1880s, the Arizona Indians often raided the territory of the Mexicans. When too closely followed by the armed forces of that country they returned to the U.S. The Apaches also made use of the passes into Mexico to evade our cavalry. Near Huachuca were several easy routes through the mountains to Mexico, and although the Indian raiding days were over and no one expected or believed the Mexicans intended attacking the United States the post remained, and still remains, rebuilt and enlarged.

Once more our much traveled goods and chattels were uncrated and unpacked and fitted into another army home. Again we were back in the kerosene age and lamps, extra wicks, oil cans, and cleaning cloths had to be accumulated. Before we left in 1916 the electric power house was up, the buildings were wired, but the "juice" had not yet been produced. Unlike Forts Assiniboine, Montana, Clark, Texas, and Stotsenburg, P.I., this post possessed a modern sanitary system and hot and cold bathtubs.

Marion and Parmelee arrived from New York and well before Christmas, 1913, we were all comfortably settled in half of a rather dilapidated set of old quarters. Captain (W.P. 1900) and Mrs. James Huston lived in the other half of the house and they were grand neighbors. Both families had the front door and hall in common and, although they had no children at that time, never once did they complain of the noise that a six-year-old boy just must make at times. Colonel Joseph F. Huston (W.P. 1873) visited his son and daughter-in-law for several weeks in 1914. The old gentleman, like so many army officers who have retired, apparently could not sleep after 4:00 or 5:00 a.m. Many times I have heard the front door gently closed as the colonel slipped out for his before sun-up constitutional. I often wondered what the sentinels, the provost sergeant and the early fatigue parties used to say when this retired regimental commander, entirely helpless to have things done his way, watched them at their duties or work.

North of the post, the foothills of the Huachuca Mountains gave way to a broad almost treeless plain that sloped gently down for several miles then gradually rose to the high peaks of the Santa Catalina range. On this plain, dry farming was being given a chance to prove its worth by, I suspect, farmers having little knowledge of the theory and practice so necessary for success in arid or semi-arid districts. Under the arid conditions that exist in this high, cool atmosphere it takes some 750 pounds of water to produce one pound of dry matter such as wheat or corn. The soil should be deep and of sandy or silty loams. Deep to hold the rains that must fall at some time of the year, sandy and silt to let the plant roots get down to draw in the moisture by capillary attraction. But in this particular vicinity and possibly due to the nature of the soil and the slope of the entire area, when the infrequent rains came they did more harm than good—often washing away the entire topsoil on these Arizona farms. Weeks of labor gone in a few moments. Certainly the area never appealed to me as an agricultural district.

3

With the Mexican civil war still going on, it wasn't long before the border towns were again calling for federal troops. In February, 1914, my troop was ordered to Yuma, Arizona, by rail. Upon arrival I found some Arizona National Guard infantry guarding the irrigation dam in the Colorado above Yuma, also part of the main irrigation ditches that spread the muddy water of the Colorado over the marvelous fertile soil south of Yuma, which this river had deposited so abundantly.

The town authorities gave us a large town lot, around the edge of which grew tall cottonwood trees, as a site for our camp. The mayor seemed quite convinced that one or the other of the Mexican combatants would come over the border, raid the farms south of Yuma and damage the irrigation dam and its ditches. He had picked out a large number of places for me to guard; but as the strength of the troop was only some seventy men I had no intention of distributing that number all over the area. I told the mayor that my job was to keep the Mexicans on their side of the border and this I would do; but if he was worried about the irrigation ditches and the water gates he would have to hire guards, as I couldn't and wouldn't disperse my small command for any such purpose. If you will look at a map of Arizona you will see that Yuma is on the left bank of the Colorado six miles above the point on the right bank where California and Mexico meet. If you continue on down the left bank of the river you are still in Arizona, while across the river is Mexico. One actually does not reach the soil of Mexico for twenty miles. This long Arizona border, as well as a small part of the desert California-Mexican border, was my real responsibility. Although I felt quite certain that the Mexicans had no idea of invading either Yuma or any portion of the surrounding country, patrols were established and I notified headquarters southern department, Fort Sam Houston, Texas, that if they wished the irrigation system guarded, a company of infantry should be sent to Yuma. This was done and I turned that job over to the company commander.

The climate of Yuma, one hundred and forty-two feet above sea level, during February, March and April, was delightful. In May the weather warmed up and by June and from then on life for anything but a Gila monster was almost unbearable.

Passengers on the air-cooled trains of today probably appreciate the difference between the temperature provided by nature and the home-made article of man, but to realize fully what the native has to bear, seven months of every year; just spend one complete twenty-four hours in a trailer, automobile, tent, or old fashioned hotel in this Arizona frying pan. The troop horses would stand for hours in the tree shade of their corral with sweat running down their legs. From about 11:00 a.m. until 3:00 or 4:00 p.m. not one of the millions of flies inhabiting the town moved unless in search of water. The soft fine dust of the roads got so hot that our mounted patrols stopped at every opportunity to stand their horses in irrigation ditches or mud puddles to cool the almost boiling heat of the hoofs and prevent dry founder.

In California across the Colorado stood the remains of the celebrated Fort Yuma of the fifties. There used to be a story in the army about a soldier who died at old Fort Yuma in the summer, went to hell, and sent back for his blanket. When I repeated this episode to an old Yuma resident he did not deny the comparative temperatures, but he contended the tale sounded false due to the fact that in Yuma no one ever owned a blanket. One day during the summer an old retired cavalryman, I believe it was Lieutenant Colonel R. D. Read (W.P. 1877), passed through town. Thinking these little brain waves on the heat waves of Yuma might amuse him, I repeated these stories. But my good intentions were entirely wasted. Turning to me he said, "Now, captain, that remark about no one ever having a blanket in Yuma is quite untrue; you and I both know that soldiers are always issued blankets no matter where they may be stationed." Oh! Well, it must have been the weather.

Due to the type of road to be encountered, Colonel Read had especially equipped his automobile for the fifty-mile desert trip between Yuma and Calexico or El Centro or any town in the Imperial Valley. After crossing the Colorado the traveler passes from the green alfalfa fields of Arizona into a small Sahara Desert. Hollywood recognized the possibilities long before the day of the sound moving pictures. Given a few camels, extras properly clothed in the turban and burnoose, no audience could guess and no Californian would dare suggest that the huge sand hills and waterless wastes were part of the Golden State.

Upon these constantly shifting sands a plank road had been constructed. It consisted of regular railroad sleepers upon which two rails were nailed made of twelve-inch planks while, to help the motor driver keep his car on the track, a low beam was fastened to the outside of each rail. Every mile or so there was a sidetrack to allow cars to pass, but it was necessary to keep a sharp watch to the front in order not to meet another car between sidetracks. To negotiate portions of this plank road that might be covered with wind-blown sand, and also to get wheel traction when long stretches of muddy roads were encountered, Read had securely fastened to the back end of each of the car's mud guards a twenty-five foot length of canvas about twelve inches wide. When the car stalled in sand or mud, he ran the canvas forward by digging out under the wheels, then on this temporary foundation he would attempt to gain sufficient momentum to send the vehicle through the remaining obstruction, with the car's coat tails streaming out behind.

As one makes the trip today over a broad concrete road, only an occasional glimpse of the wreck of the old plank road reminds the "old motor timers" of the navigational expedients of those early automobile tours.

Over all our sleeping tents, as well as the long tarpaulin covered men's mess tent, we placed light branches full of green leaves—renewing them as the leaves faded. Drill for men not on guard or patrol duty was held early in the morning. All the men were taught to swim and all the horses we required to swim in the wide, deep main irrigation ditches. We practiced transporting two or three men and all the equipment they carried on themselves and their mounts on small rafts made of light branches strapped to supports made of the individual shelter halves filled with grass or weeds and tightly rolled into canvas buoys. With mess cans used as paddles, C Troop could have crossed even the Colorado River, except when in flood.

The water from the Colorado, which filled these big irrigation ditches (actually rivers some fifty or sixty feet wide and ten or twelve feet deep), is so full of silt that it looks more like mud than water. If a swimmer went a quarter of an inch below the surface he completely disappeared. While swimming instruction of the beginners was in progress, I was always fearful of drowning one of the men. Gerstner, a crack swimmer, was in charge, and one day as feared a man disappeared—one of the qualified swimmers. The instruction was being held in a main ditch near one of the gates that controlled the flow of water into a subsidiary ditch that carried the water to a farm. When we about gave up hope I found that dead beating soldier had dived under the side gate, which was drawn up a foot or two, and was quietly sitting in the shade on the other side. Although I was mad enough to then drown him, my relief at his discovery rather neutralized my remarks.

From a rebellion point of view nothing happened in the seven months we occupied Yuma. Once a wild telephone message came from some farm, several miles south of us, that a large body of Mexican irregular cavalry had crossed the Arizona-Mexico border and were advancing towards Yuma. I sent my first lieutenant, Louis A. O'Donnell (W.P. 1905), with ten men to investigate, he returned and reported the whole story a fake. Of course the good American citizens living on or near the Mexican border are certainly entitled to protection. In my opinion they were entitled to much better protection than they ever received at Calexico, California, in 1911; Naco, Arizona, in 1914–16, just to mention two border towns I know about personally. But even a troop of cavalry is financially not an unwelcome tourist in a small town. That view of the question produced strange and terrible dreams in the sleep of local mayors or chambers of commerce. Their restless minds saw pillage and death creeping towards them from the border; not long afterward what should turn up but the cavalry or infantry.

Marion and Parmelee came down from five thousand foot Huachuca to Yuma for a visit. I rented a little wooden house near my troop camp and we tried keeping house—rather more like camping out—for a month. The change from cool Huachuca to stifling Yuma was too much for our small son, and he and Marion went off by train to visit the grandparents in Ross Valley, California.

With some seventy men and an equal number of horses in camp in a hot town with myriad flies, the sanitary condition of our entire camp was vital. We built dry earth closets and homemade shower baths for both officers and the enlisted men. An adobe built trash and food incinerator that, even today, could be copied with advantage by many towns without proper garbage disposal. The last formation of the day was Retreat under arms, when the Officer of the Day made a careful inspection of rifles and pistols; then supper.

One hot day in September, I visited what was left of old Fort Yuma across the river in California. The military post of Yuma was established in 1850 to protect the emigrants of southern California from the attacks of hostile Indians. On November 27, 1850, Brevet Major S. P. Heintzelman (W.P. 1826), captain, 2nd Infantry, received instructions from headquarters of the tenth military district, Monterey, California, to establish a post somewhere near the junction of the Gila with the Colorado. The camp was first established on the bottom near what was known as the old ferry crossing about a half mile below the junction of the two rivers, but was moved in March, 1851, to the top of the bluff on the site of an old Spanish mission said to have been in operation in the year 1700. Owing to the scarcity of supplies and the difficulty of obtaining provisions, the camp was abandoned in June, 1851. On the twenty-ninth of February, 1852, Major Heintzelman returned and re-established a permanent garrison. This post although not the most southerly was the hottest military post in the U.S., a temperature of 100 degrees may exist for weeks in succession. Fort Yuma was transferred from the control and jurisdiction of the War Department to that of the Interior Department on July 22, 1884.

As I sat in the hot shade of my tent, watching the flies suck water from the sides of my canvas water bucket, it occurred to me that I might amuse myself and perhaps some bored adjutant general along what was known as "military channels" by submitting a seriously worded letter recommending that the Congress be asked, by the President, to enact the necessary legislation to enable the Chief Executive to award the living members of old Fort Yuma (if there were any) a medal to commemorate their service in that forsaken spot, and if all had passed on, then to their nearest living relatives. After considerable thought I concocted a letter that I felt sure would startle even the old army War Department clerks if it managed to progress that far up the channel. Three days after mailing my facetious epistle I received a telegram ordering C Troop back to Fort Huachuca. And so, after five months of tent life in a place that really never needed us, someone had remembered where we were and graciously sent us home.

Odd as it may seem, it isn't very difficult to get lost in the army. I do not mean lost to the extent that not even the record clerks know where an organization can be found, but lost or forgotten by one's military superiors to such an extent that they have forgotten when the organization went to some station, why it went, and why it is still there.

To follow the trail of my old Fort Yuma letter I must add the following. Seven years after the letter had been mailed, I was going by train from Washington to Philadelphia when across the car aisle I saw an old friend of my father's, Colonel R. A. Brown (W.P. 1885), cavalry. In 1914, Brown was a major and the chief of staff of the southern department commanded by General Bliss.

Colonel Brown said to me, "Conrad, do you remember a letter you wrote in Yuma a long time ago, about medals for old Fort Yuma survivors?"

"Yes," I replied, "I remember that fool letter."

"Well," continued the colonel, "the morning that crazy communication arrived General Bliss happened to be in a very good humor, so thinking it might amuse him I took it in and showed it to him. He read it, laughed and said, "Order that young man back to his post."

Five

Soissons I

On the morning of July 15, 1918, I left Paris and, in the afternoon, rejoined the 18th Infantry, which had moved to the Forêt de Compiègne. There I learned that the division was scheduled for an early attack against the enemy's entrenched position west of Soissons and south of the Aisne River. There was a rumor that I was to be assigned to command the 28th Infantry to replace Colonel Hanson E. Ely, just appointed a brigadier general. Nothing was official; division headquarters sent no advanced information or an order to confer with the commanding officer of the 28th Infantry.

On the morning of the sixteenth, at Colonel Parker's direction, I went out and thoroughly inspected the roads and trails leading to that portion of the then held French entrenched line, which was to be taken over by the 18th Infantry. Upon my return to Parker's headquarters I gave him a full account of the area his regiment was to occupy. The next morning, the seventeenth of July, I received Special Order 195, headquarters, First Division, dated July 16, 1918, directing me to assume command of the 28th Infantry.

The colonel was Frank Parker, not John H. ("Gatling Gun") Parker.

1

During the night of July 16–17 the 28th Infantry had marched from its bivouac in the Forêt de Compiègne to some woods near Mortefontaine, and there, about 1:00 p.m., July 17, I found that regiment's headquarters and took command. Shortly after joining my new command all brigade and regimental commanders were ordered to report to the division commander, Major General Charles P. Summerall, for a conference. General Summerall had been commanding the artillery brigade of the First Division; but a day or two before had replaced General Robert L. Bullard as division commander. These changes gave the division, the artillery, and the 28th Infantry new commanders almost on the very day of the contemplated offensive. In my case, the change was made just 16 hours before the regiment went into battle. These are examples of how little our G.H.Q. cared about who commanded troops in battle.

July 1918, was not the first time Mortefontaine appeared in American history. A century and more earlier, September 30, 1800, representatives of the United States signed a treaty of Mortefontaine with Napoleon at what then was the country estate of Joseph Bonaparte, Napoleon's brother. The treaty abrogated the alliance of 1778 with France, so necessary for the success of the American Revolution. In return the U.S. gave up claims for spoliations from France incurred during the European wars since 1793. It was part of Napoleon's scheme for an Armed Neutrality, an organization of Europe's neutrals against Great Britain.

As General Summerall's, after the battle, treatment of me was, in my opinion, unfair and completely undeserved, I warn my readers that even today, twenty-four years after the battle, I still resent his action, and admit that I bear him great dislike and am entirely out of accord with those who consider him a great war leader.

At the division conference the division attack order was gone over. General Summerall personally repeated the words of the written order, Field Order No. 27, headquarters, First Division, July 16, 1918, that the infantry would attack in the "normal formation." This formation had been taught the division during the winter 1917–18. As this formation was largely responsible for the terrible casualties suffered by the infantry in the Battle of Soissons, I will explain it in detail.

The infantry companies had four platoons; and while the enlisted strength of a company was 250 men, it is probable that none of the platoons went into action with more than 50 men. As formed for the attack, the 50-man platoon, commanded by a lieutenant, was divided into two sections, each section under a sergeant. The leading or assault platoon deployed one section (25 men) as skirmishers, at four or five paces interval between men, on a front of about 125 yards. The second section (25 men) followed the skirmishers at a distance of about 50 yards in a formation that is called a "line of squad columns," which means a line of three squads (8 men to a squad) going forward as directed by the squad leader (a corporal). On the 125 yard front each squad had a space about 40 yards in width in which to operate without interfering with other squads to its right or left. Another platoon of the same company followed 150 or 200 yards behind; this platoon was formed into two sections, each section formed as described of the rear section of the assault platoon. The distance between the two sections was 50 yards. The other two platoons of the same company were formed to the right or left, in a similar manner and on a frontage of 125 yards. This formation thus assembled some 200 men in an area 250 yards wide, and at a maximum of 300 yards deep (front to rear).

Another company was similarly formed to the right or left, in prolongation of the company, above described. The remaining two companies followed the leading companies at a distance of from 300 to 500 yards, their platoons being formed as described for the support platoon of the leading company. The entire battalion of some 800 men occupied an area approximately 500 yards wide (right to left) and from 600 to 800 yards deep (front to rear).

Immediately behind the two leading companies came Company C, 2nd Machine Gun Battalion with 12 machine guns. Of the 36 machine guns which followed the battalions of the regiment into action, 19 were destroyed. One company lost all their officers and as far as I was able to learn did little firing.

About 500 yards in rear of the rear elements of the leading battalion came the support battalion, formed in line of platoon columns or line of section columns on the same width of front as the organization they followed. Actually this compact formation put two battalions, a maximum of 2,000 men, but in this fight each not over 1,000 men, in an area 500 yards by 1,700 yards; but of all this number only 100 men (four sections) were occupying the front line where they could fire while 1,500 men acted as backstops for the enemy's bullets.

The machine guns were carried forward. A man carried the barrel, another the trail, other members of the squad carried ammunition or other essential parts of the machine. No one can crawl or creep very far with a heavy load on his shoulder, nor can he do much running on a hot July day in a thick field of growing wheat. Consequently these machine guns, which could not fire from their assigned positions (unless they found ground sufficiently high to let them fire over the infantry in front of them) just had to follow and take it. A man carrying a machine gun barrel or trail was a conspicuous object. To knock out an unassembled machine gun or mortar it isn't necessary to kill or wound a majority of the crew. All that is needed is to wound the man carrying the barrel or the trail; or, in the case of the mortar, the iron base, or for either weapon, the ammunition carriers. Unless arrangements have been made to assemble and check losses at points accurately decided upon before the attack, there is little chance of finding missing parts.

As for the automatic rifles (the French Chauchat), with but one or two exceptions, this easily jammed and complicated piece of mechanism was soon discarded by the automatic riflemen for the old reliable U.S. Springfield rifle, taken from men killed or wounded. Our army has recently (1941) adopted and is arming all riflemen with the automatic Garand rifle. I predict that if our troops use it in this war it will be the cause of hundreds, perhaps thousands, of men being unable to fire their rifles as automatics in an emergency. Only a well trained, careful man, devoted to the care of his rifle, can keep an automatic rifle or gun in operation under the stress and excitement of battle.

The Chauchat light machine gun probably was, as the author of a machine gun book appraised it, the worst gun on the Western Front. The excellent Browning guns, light and heavy, only began to become available near the end of World War I.

Where several divisions were making a simultaneous attack, the brigades, regiments, battalions, companies and platoons had to exercise great care to keep in their allotted area and move straight towards their own immediate part of the general objective. If the assault platoons meandered from their correct line of advance, they immediately got in front or rear of their comrades to the right or left. In these cases they either masked the fire of that organization or were unable to fire themselves, and in both cases left the enemy, in their own sector, unopposed. So it was very necessary to have the assault platoons move directly towards their own objectives. This was accomplished by either using a watch compass bearing or by keeping two well defined natural objects, such as trees, church steeples, or houses in line. In each company the platoon commanders were responsible that this was done; but as they had to see that the two sections of their platoons kept up the fight and the advance, the keeping on the line of advance had to be done, actually, by one or more men in the front line of skirmishers. If, in an attack, these guides did not become casualties, and if they were thoroughly reliable and courageous men, the general direction of the assault platoons could be fairly well maintained. The whole idea was purely theoretical and rested on too many "ifs."

It must be remembered that the French taught the First Division this attack formation. When the French prescribed it, they were thinking of an attack against an objective, possibly two or three hundred yards away, perhaps even less. In France, during the fortress warfare of 1915 to 1918, the assault battalions, support battalions and reserves jumped off from deep trenches. By the time the first wave (assault platoon) had reached the enemy firing trenches, into which they jumped, the second wave had emerged from their jump-off trench. Therefore, what with their own trench system and that of the enemy, the attackers were not all above ground at the same time; but when the final objective was a mile to several miles distant, this compact attack formation, led by skirmishers, resulted in great losses and maintaining direction became impossible.

The field order prescribed that the two infantry brigades would attack abreast with their regiments abreast, each regiment to have one battalion in the front line, one in support. The two interior third line battalions became the brigade reserve (one for each brigade), while the two exterior battalions the division reserve. The artillery was to lay down a rolling barrage, the cadence of which was to be 100 meters in 3 minutes.

What the French called a groupement (4 groups of 3 batteries of 4 tanks 48 in all) were to advance with the infantry.

The post of command of the 2nd Infantry Brigade was in a dugout on a trail 600 meters east of Riverseau Farm; and the 28th Infantry P.C. was in the woods 300 meters east of the Le Chauffeur. When I got there after 10:00 p.m. it was still occupied by part of a French battalion headquarters, I think it was, of the regiment we were relieving. My almost new trench coat was stolen that evening, by, I always suspected, a French soldier but I may be mistaken.

The French entrenched front line was just east of the valley in which Laverine, Le Chauffeur and Cutry were located, and ran approximately north and south. Our direction of attack was a little south of east, Raparie and Croix Ste. Creande being about 300 yards north of our north regimental boundary. From Cutry to Le Mont d'Arly and the Missy-aux-Bois ravine, the country is almost level and generally covered with wheat. From the Saint-Amand Farm, the country road leads down to Le Mont d'Arly, and in the almost perpendicular ridge to the east of the road there were several large grottos or underground stone quarries with entrances just wide enough for a two horse wagon to enter. There is a creek in the bottom of the 1,000 yard wide ravine. The floor of the valley was heavily wooded and in the center of it a deep swamp. Then across the ravine from Mont d'Arly is the stone village of Breuil, built on the side of the steep east bank and on the level ground above. 1,400 yards south of Breuil and built on the plateau just south of the ravine was the stone village of Missy-aux-Bois. From there to Ploisy, about one and three-quarter miles east, is another wheat covered plateau. Ploisy is built in the bottom of another steep and wide ravine, the sides of which were heavily wooded. The Ploisy ravine extended north and east for several hundred yards, then turned sharply to the right, ran due south and there was the fairly large and closely built stone village of Berzy le Sec. Between Ploisy and Berzy le Sec is a flat plain of 1,200 yards, perfectly open, and at that time only grass covered.

In the bottom of the Berzy le Sec ravine was a railroad that formerly ran to Villers-Cotterets, also a good motor road. From the high ground east of this ravine, the enemy had direct observation of any movement made east of Ploisy or between Ploisy and Missy-aux-Bois. Likewise, from the north, towards Soissons, enemy artillery could easily see us.

After the division conference I returned to the headquarters of the 28th Infantry and went over, in as much detail as possible, the part we were to play in the coming battle. Except as a division staff officer during the previous winter, I was unknown to my regiment as they were to me. Due to the Bastile Day review, all the battalion commanders were still absent, also some 250 men twenty belonging to each of the twelve companies.

The battalion commanders did not return until three hours before the regiment started the march to the front line; and the composite company not until 7:00 p.m. General Ely had gone and Lieutenant Colonel J. M. Cullison (1899) was in temporary command. Apparently no attempt had been made to make a reconnaissance of the territory between Mortefontaine and the French position. The last and only time I saw Colonel Cullison, after our first meeting about 2:00 p.m. on the seventeenth, was the next morning about 10:00 a.m. (six hours after the battle began). He complained of having a lame ankle and that he couldn't walk much more. I ordered him back to the rear echelon at Laversine to assist in forwarding supplies to the regiment. He remained there during the rest of the battle.

Considering how Babcock was appointed at the last minute to command of the 28th Regiment, his list of further command thoughtlessness is astonishing. All the battalion commanders, and a large contingent of troops, absent on July 14 at the Paris Bastile Day parade!

The 28th Infantry left the western side of the little town of Mortefontaine at 9:00 p.m., July 17, following French soldier guides. The French front lines were about eight miles distant; but, in order to relieve road congestion as much as possible, the companies had to follow trails across fields pitted with shell holes. These were very muddy and to add to the difficulties it rained and the night was very dark. Marching through the mud was slow and tiring, and the men had to follow one another in single file. To keep the long column from being broken or parts of it getting lost in the darkness, men often held on to some part of the equipment of the man in front. The confusion in and around Le Chauffeur and Laversine, caused by outgoing French troops and incoming French tanks, was very great blocking the streets and roads.

The assault battalion (Second), commanded by Major Clarence R. Huebner (1916), reached the jump-off position about 4:15 a.m., twenty minutes before the hour for the attack; the support battalion (Third), commanded by Major Willis J. Tack (1914), was in position about ten minutes before H hour 4:35 a.m., July 18.

Babcock could not have found a better battalion commander than Huebner, who apart from the colonel commanding was the regiment's

mainstay. Huebner proved one of the outstanding American officers in Europe in World War II, reaching the rank of lieutenant general. He took command of the First Division in Sicily, led it into Normandy, and then led V Corps.

After a more than seven-hour, night mud march, our gallant soldiers were about to engage in the most sanguinary battle fought by the First Division during the war. I, with the forward echelon of headquarters, followed a guide to the French dugout east of Le Chauffeur. General Beaumont Buck had directed that I establish a chain of messengers (runners) from my P.C. to his. This was done, and it required the services of twelve men. During the night, the regimental signal detachment established a telephone line between my P.C. and the brigade P.C.

Promptly at 4:35 a.m., the combined American and French artillery barrage started, and word came back from Major Huebner that his battalion was advancing. On our left was the 153rd French Division, and on the right the other regiment of the 2nd Brigade, the 26th Infantry, commanded by Colonel Hamilton A. Smith (W.P. 1891).

2

Although in all the regimental training maneuvers the regimental commander sat in his P.C. and endeavored to keep track of his regiment's progress by telephone to the battalion commanders or, failing that mechanical means of communication, by runner, that was not and still is not my idea of how to assist the battalion commanders, or keep in touch with conditions at the front. In the French Army and I believe in the British Army also, even the battalion commanders established P. C.'s far to the rear of their firing lines hoping to keep in touch by runner or telephone with the captains commanding the fighting companies.

So, about 5:00 a.m., being unable to see what was going on and receiving no further word from Huebner, I left the dugout, leaving Lieutenant S. W. Marshall, National Army, the operations officer of the regiment, to maintain communication with the brigade. As I went to the front, the first of our wounded as well as German prisoners were passed, going to the rear. One wounded American soldier was being carried on a litter by four prisoners. One of them, a nice looking little Boche who didn't look a day over eighteen, smiled and chanted in the gayest manner, "La guerre est fini," repeating it over and over, at the same time imitating the "passage steps" of a dressage or trained horse. That man was certainly glad to be a prisoner. The German prisoners did not mind holding their arms up. I saw many of them running to our rear with their arms held as high as possible; they made me think of a young bird trying to fly.

In World War I the U.S. Army created a fiction, the National Army, meaning either the enlisted or draft members. The Regular Army made officers' commissions or promotions in the National Army, meaning that at war's end those commissions or promotions also would end.

Going forward just in rear of the support battalion, I saw a French tank being actually chased by shells. Apparently some German gunner of 77-mm. cannon was in a position to fire directly on this tank. When one of the shells hit right in front, the tank turned and sought safety in a little hollow where it seemed to be out of sight of the German gunner. Several of the little Renaults were put out of action by hits from machine guns, placed where direct and accurate fire could be brought to bear on attacking tanks.

The battlefield was in general level and covered with growing wheat between four and five feet high. The rifle and machine gun fire was continuous, but the German artillery was not firing heavily. I could see the clouds of smoke and dirt thrown up by our barrage, but even it was not the dense hail of falling shells one imagines a barrage to be, and that the artillerymen think they are laying down. Later my regiment was supported by only the First Battalion of the 7th Field Artillery, commanded by Major Francis A. Ruggles (1901).

When I left the P.C. near Le Chauffeur, the P.C. was automatically moved forward with me. The regimental signal detail attempted to maintain telephone communication, via the old P.C., with the brigade P.C. The wire furnished us was a drum or two of very large telephone wire, which two men carried on a pole passed through the center of the drum. It was a very heavy load, cumbersome, and the detail could not keep up with me; but in spite of these difficulties the line was brought up, about 2:00 p.m. to the next temporary post of command at Le Mont d'Arly. There was no wire or equipment to run a line forward to the front line battalion commander, about eleven hundred yards away near a small farm called Breuil.

Prior to my arrival at Le Mont d'Arly, I halted regimental headquarters in a field just south of a ruined mill called St. Amand. Here the signal officer attempted to use two different sets of apparatus, one designated as the T.P.S. (telephone through the ground), the other T.S.F. (telephone without wire). Both were of French manufacture. Either due to defective parts or to a shell that hit within fifty feet of us, throwing dirt in all directions, neither of these affairs functioned during the battle. I used the good old runner, the courageous infantry soldier messenger, between myself and the battalion commanders and back to the regimental P.C. when I was in advance of it. Runners to the battalions were men from the battalions. Sent to my headquarters by battalion commanders, these men knew where to go to deliver messages.

Artillery liaison officers were attached to the staff of the battalion and regimental staffs; and by means of artillery runners, or by the personal efforts of these officers, a certain amount of contact was maintained with the artillery. I remember, however, that on the morning of July 19 it took several hours to get artillery fire concentrated on a line of enemy machine guns, located east of Breuil near the Soissons-Paris road.

But to get back to the early morning fighting on the eighteenth. Eight French (Renault) tanks were assigned to cooperate with my regiment. I saw two or three of them that morning; they were either not operating or running for cover and in any event were too far behind the firing line to be of any use. I do not know what the other five may have done; do not remember hearing anything about them, except one which assisted in capturing many Germans that had taken refuge in one of the caverns near Le Mont d'Arly.

The light Renault two-man tank was a failure. Armed with a machine gun or a 35-mm. cannon, the tank lacked speed. It could go five or six miles an hour, which enabled any artillery piece to hole it. The German antitank rifle, a huge squirrel rifle three times the caliber of an ordinary rifle, operated with a tripod, was quite effective.

The first and second objectives were captured promptly, but the losses in the assault and support battalions were very heavy. By the time

Huebner's battalion had taken the second objective, the high ground about 200 meters east of the Montplaiser Farm, at 9:30 a.m., all its officers had been killed or wounded, except Huebner, who was wounded the next day. The loss among the enlisted men was very heavy. Huebner reported that he had organized his battalion under noncommissioned officers. The support battalion, under Tack who was wounded, lost all but twelve of its officers and many men before they had fired a shot.

In the advance towards the first objective there was a farm held and fortified by the enemy some 300 yards to the north of our area, and should have been taken by the French; but as that had not been done, Major Huebner directed Second Lieutenant Jim Quinn, National Army, to capture it with his platoon. This gallant officer accomplished his mission promptly, captured a hundred Germans and five machine guns. For this action Quinn was awarded the Distinguished Service Cross.

When the two leading companies (H and G) reached the Missy-aux-Bois ravine, the other two companies (E and F) were brought up on the left and at the same time three companies of the support battalion (Third) were put in on the left of Huebner's battalion. With these seven decimated companies, the attack carried the swampy ravine to the second objective east of the Montplaiser Farm. In this advance of 3–1/8 miles over the shell and machine gun swept wheat fields, down through and up the very steep ravine between Missy-aux-Bois and Breuil, the assault battalion had swung too much to the north (left). About 11:00 a.m., I inspected the front lines east and southeast of Breuil and found that the regiment was occupying ground supposed to be in the French sector. I hunted up the French battalion commander in Breuil and told him I intended moving my troops out of his sector. The object of this was to advance in our own area with the greatly reduced strength of the combined Second and Third battalions. The French commander requested me not to do this, giving as his reason his losses and inability to hold more ground. He was no worse off than we were. Finally we selected a cross in a field due east of the southern end of Breuil as marking a point on the east and west dividing line between the 28th and the French infantry.

I have forgotten the regimental number of the French infantry on our left on the eighteenth of July, but it appeared to be composed of native Algerians and Tunisians. As I walked down behind their front line, which was holding the high bank of a country road, I greeted them in my poor

French. One tall, swarthy fellow responded and recognizing me as an American said, "How many battles have you been in?" I replied that this was my first battle in this war. He tapped his Croix de Guerre ribbon and, in a patronizing tone, enumerated the battles he had seen.

In some way, and very naturally, many conflicts wear off the keen zest and often careless courage of the novice. The French regiment to our left with its three war years and many conflicts could not keep up to the gallant 28th; and, in consequence, we suffered from the left flanking fire of the enemy from the jump-off to the last assault.

After the American-French regimental boundary line was fixed, I directed Huebner to withdraw the remnants of this fine battalion to the west and rear of Tack's battalion, and to organize it in depth. This was done gradually and under all available cover, and was accomplished without loss.

Of course the barrage had long since left us. Major Huebner reported it was impossible to keep up with it from the start. On the second objective the advance of the 28th and 26th infantries had been stopped. Our losses were tremendous. The officers told me that after crossing the Missy-aux-Bois ravine the men were exhausted and the attack died out. That was about 9:30 a.m. For twelve hours these men had been marching or fighting or both without any sleep and hardly a moment of rest. What food they had they carried. After a seven-hour night march in the mud and rain, they had been fighting and crawling and walking or running through heavy fields of wheat, a swamp waist-deep in places. The two battalions had lost about 70 percent of their personnel in killed and wounded, and all the officers but Major Huebner in the Second Battalion and more than 50 percent in the Third Battalion.

Now I will tell why we had such unprecedented battle losses. In the first place and more than any other cause was the formation, already described, an area too full of men. With the flat trajectory of the modern rifle and machine gun bullet, there is a long narrow danger zone from front to rear. Bullets missing the front line soldier could and did go on to hit someone beyond. It is entirely possible that the same bullet may have wounded more than one man.

Then, in addition, the high standing wheat had much to do with the loss. To go forward the men had to stand up to see where they were going and, of course, to shoot. All over the battle area I saw the steel helmets of the men as they laboriously waded through the thick wheat. Men seriously wounded, unable to call for help or move about, were very difficult to find, and in all probability some died in those wheat fields who might have recovered had they been found.

Through these high thick fields of wheat the Germans had mowed swaths running parallel to their firing lines. These lanes were about 100 yards wide and extended fully across the regimental area. On the east side of these lanes German machine gunners and automatic riflemen had dug holes in the wheat fields about a yard or two back from the edge of the cleared lane. These holes were about three feet square and seven or eight feet deep. In them they had a narrow ladder, and the dirt removed had been carefully scattered. As soon as the barrage rolled past, the men could climb the ladder, poke their machine gun or automatic rifle up to the edge of the standing wheat and, well hidden, take up perfect positions to fire on the hundreds of steel hats that they could see advancing through the wheat. Once our men reached the mowed section they also took shelter along their edge of the lane. Then it became a matter of locating the enemy opposite and, with the support of hot rifle fire directed on the spot where he seemed to be located, running men across the swath to outflank, kill or capture him. This took lots of time, was deadly work. In the meantime the 100 yards every 3-minute advance of the barrage went on its way. The chance that the light barrage, behind which we were supposed to be attacking, would drop a shell down one of these enemy holes or near enough to bury the occupants was very slight. I saw no indication of it anywhere. Only the courage and individual initiative of the soldiers of this fine regiment enabled them, at terrible cost, to cross these numerous death dealing zones.

I was standing talking with two officers in the center of one of these captured swaths, some four or five hundred yards behind our front line, when there was the crack of a rifle discharge near at hand as a bullet went through the fleshy lower part of one leg of the artillery officer serving on my staff. Some wounded or not yet captured German had, I believe, fired on us from nearby. It was almost useless to hunt for him in the mass of stubble and standing grain. Even if we found him, all he had to do was lie still and play dead. We just moved out of that particular area.

During the five-day battle, the 28th Infantry lost 58 officers and 1,760 men killed or wounded. An officer loss of over 60 percent and an enlisted man loss of more than 46 percent. Actually, the percentage of casualties was far greater, as it is based on the authorized strength of a regiment, 3,806 men; whereas the regiment was below strength and the vast majority of casualties fell on the twelve infantry companies and the three machine gun companies.

In the almost perpendicular west side of Le Mont d'Arly and Missy-aux-Bois ravine are several huge caves. Sometime after 10:00 a.m. I established the regimental P.C. in one of them, and about 2:00 p.m. wire communication was made with General Buck's headquarters. The headquarters of the French regiment on our left came in sometime later. Both the 28th and the French used a nearby cave as a first aid station. As men died they were laid outside awaiting burial, while dozens of stretcher cases covered the floor of this cool almost pitch-dark cavern. It was a ghastly spot.

A short distance south of our cavern there was another one; and while our men were advancing across the swampy ravine towards Breuil, many bullets were noticed coming from behind them. At first it was thought that German snipers were firing from treetops, but upon investigation it was discovered that the firing was coming from the mouth of one of these caves. Many German officers and enlisted men had taken refuge in the cave south of us when our men appeared through the wheat on the edge of the cliff. For six or seven hours that morning and afternoon, Captain John S. Manning and his company, E, attempted to get them out. The Germans continued to fire on our men across the valley, and although Manning rounded up a French tank and persuaded the crew to take it into the mouth of the cave and there fire their small cannon, the enemy refused to surrender. Finally, about 6:00 p.m., the senior officers in the cave wrote a note of surrender, stuck it on a pole and had it shoved out to some American soldier who was stationed near the entrance but out of the line of fire. The openings to these caves faced east toward the enemy; a dirt road led past them, sloping down to the bottom of the ravine. Out of this cave came a major, twenty other officers and, as I now remember, nearly 100 enlisted men. Captain Manning marched them down under guard to my P.C. with this long column of men standing in sight of the enemy artillery. I was afraid it might open fire on them, not knowing who they were, but nothing happened. I directed that each prisoner be searched for weapons. The German major was a Prussian. I was told he was a relative of the German crown prince. It was amusing to see those haughty officers when one of our husky, sweaty, dirty soldiers frisked them for arms. We even took their dirks or daggers, although they claimed they were only for mess purposes. I do not suppose any of those Prussians had ever before had an ordinary man lay hands on him, unless it was to help with his coat or pull on his trousers.

One of our surgeons, I think it was the regimental surgeon, suggested that there might be hospital corps men among them that we could use to assist our men in searching the wheat fields for the wounded of both sides. So, I asked the group of German officers if any of them spoke English. Not one answered. Then I explained what was wanted and at once a big, fine looking young fellow admitted he understood English. He stepped out, went along the column and in a few moments brought back 25 or 30 men, each one wearing on his sleeve the Red Cross mark of the medical branch. These men, under guard, were then turned over to the regimental surgeon, and as I now remember brought in many wounded Americans and Germans. After searching all the caves, about 170 more men, several horses, a wagon and tons of equipment were found. I sent the prisoners, 604 of them, back on the road toward Laversine under the guard of 20 infantrymen.

Until darkness fell on this first day of the battle, there were too many things to do to sleep. In fact, although I had not slept a wink for over thirty-six hours and had nothing to eat but a sandwich for 24 hours, neither of these usually considered deprivations seemed to bother me. There was too much responsibility and excitement. Had I been a more experienced regimental commander and known the supply officer, food would have come up after dark of the eighteenth, but nothing came, not even ambulances, which worried me far more than food.

Six

Soissons II

1

At 3:50 a.m., July 19, I was roused from a heavy sleep on the dirt floor of our immense cavern and handed a long typewritten order from the brigade to attack at 4:00 a.m.; along with a mass of useless information to us was the important item that for forty-five minutes or until 4:45 a.m. the artillery barrage would "stand" on a line several hundred yards east of the Paris-Soissons road (Route Nationel No. 2 de Paris). This "stand" fire of the artillery was to fall on a line 1,500 yards east of our front line, and, in consequence, would have no effect on the enemy in the immediate proximity. Although the brigade had been notified as to the location of the front line of my regiment, and I assume this information had been transmitted to the division, no attempt was made by either of them to ascertain where artillery fire should fall to give us the greatest assistance; not a soul from either headquarters came near us.

With just ten minutes to get word to Major Tack, who had a P.C. in or near Breuil about 1,000 yards away across the ravine I spent no time considering how effective the barrage would be, nor did I write out an order. A runner was sent at once to Tack to attack at 4:00 a.m. It was probably five minutes to four when the runner left, even if he ran all the way, and it is doubtful if he ran a step over the dark trail and little narrow foot bridges in the ravine; he couldn't have reached Tack by 4:00 a.m.

Major Tack (now a lieutenant colonel) has recently written me that the sound of the 4:00 a.m. barrage awakened him, and shortly afterward "a runner who was pretty well winded, gasped out: the orders are to attack at four o'clock." Tack put his battalion in motion as quickly as possible with the verbal, "We attack at once, straight to the front, in the present formation." These orders were transmitted to his front line companies by officers. Tack notified one of the support company commanders. This battalion was already deployed in attack formation, so all the officers had to do was get their organizations moving forward. Just how far east of the Paris-Soissons road that barrage "stood" or for actually how long, I do not know; but Colonel Tack reports that they never saw the barrage. Even if the runner did run, it must have been at least 4:20 a.m. before the battalion moved.

In this same cavern was the commanding officer of the French infantry regiment on our left, which belonged to the 153rd French Division. His order to attack at 4:00 a.m. reached him at 4:10 a.m. Right on the dot at 4:00 a.m. we could hear the bursting shells of our artillery support, Major Ruggles' battalion of the 7th Field Artillery, far away to the east.

A mere recital of the American method of communication between army-corps-division-brigade-regiment-battalion and company in this battle could mean little to those who may, in future years, read these pages. Anyone who has ever commanded troops in battle will appreciate the absurdity of the staff procedure, the inefficiency of a headquarters permitting these delays, and the abysmal ignorance of infantry fighting by a commander willing to see his staff officers, stenographers and typewriting clerks make out long formal orders for an emergency operation; knowing that when they reached the brigade, that staff would extract from the first order that which applied to the brigade, then retypewrite these extracts for his two regiments and any other separate commands while the clock ticks on.

I wonder if Grant, Lee, Sherman, Jackson, Sheridan, or Stuart would have become the slave of the typewriter, with only the good old horse to speed up message delivery on the field of battle. I know of no Civil War delay to equal the transmission of Field Order No. 28 of the First Division dated July 19, 1918, with their motorcycles, automobiles, horses and telephones running all the way down to the headquarters of the regiments. One may well ask if, at the division, anyone thinks or realizes that there may be many hours between the writing of an order and its receipt by the officers and men required to put it into fighting effect.

Personally I doubt that in any headquarters where no one has commanded front line soldiers in battle, a thought is given to the matter. They are in the same class with the commanding general and staff of an American corps, visited, so the tale is told, by a war correspondent on the morning of September 12, 1918, the day of the St. Mihiel offensive. Not a soul was awake, the reporter was horrified, then he became tranquil as he remembered that "the brains of the army," having done their work, were now resting. Untroubled they slept on; their orders had been typewritten, approved, transmitted, receipted for, it was now the duty of the fighting forces to carry out their wise and well-written directions, no matter at what hour received.

In this 4:00 a.m. attack, neither the division nor the brigade had the sense to use the telephone and say, "be alert," in guarded language if deemed necessary, although under the circumstances there wasn't one chance in a million any German could cut in on the line. Of course, if the division had been under Sheridan or Stonewall Jackson, fast riding motorcycle officers might have put-putted down to all brigade and regimental P.C.'s hours before, giving commanding officers the necessary details for the attack. Even with the new aid, radio phones, I predict that front line commanders are going to meet the same criminal delays in this war.

Keeping in touch with the 26th Infantry on our left, the 28th advanced to the west edge of the Route Nationale, No.2 de Paris (Paris-Soissons road). The French on our left had reached this road at a point about 1,100 yards north of our left flank; but the country between the two regiments, assigned to the French, was still occupied by the enemy. From north of the Breuil-Ploisy road on our left, and east of the Route Number 2, came a heavy machine gun fire: the 2nd Brigade was stopped.

Part of one of our companies on the extreme left, which had captured and was occupying a shallow enemy trench, was suddenly fired upon by flanking machine guns that apparently had a clear side view of the men. Almost to a man they were instantly killed. Major Tack was wounded early in the engagement, Major Huebner taking command of both battalions.

The left flank of the 28th was refused, or bent back to the left and rear to cover the big bulge left by the French. I am very familiar with the fact that when organizations, especially those on the ends or flanks of a command, fail to carry their objectives, the excuse is nearly always blamed on the fellow to the right or left who is behind. So, unquestionably, critics of the 28th Infantry may accuse me of using the same old excuse. They would be correct. I do not blame the French regiment. We had a difficult and exceptionally bloody struggle in our own area, and no time was spent finding out whether the French difficulties were less or greater. Their start, on the morning of the nineteenth, must have been much later than ours, and for all I know their line of attack that morning may have been at a divergent angle to ours. It is quite possible that the enemy in this unconquered area had not been attacked and not only poured a devastating fire into the left flank of the 28th but treated the right flank of the French to the same medicine. And now the armchair tactician will remark that had there been close and careful liaison between the Americans and the French this enemy bulge would have been discovered at once. This too is correct. As darkness fell on the eighteenth, the lines were in contact north and east of Breuil; by 6:00 a.m. they were 1,000 yards apart.

The second day of the battle began in the dark, and no hot food had been received since leaving Mortefontaine on the seventeenth. I have never learned what the trouble was, but after dark on the eighteenth and every night thereafter I saw no reason why hot food should not have been received.

I went through the high wheat up to the front line of my regiment and down that line to the 26th Infantry where I met and talked with Colonel Smith.

During the day there were many air battles. While two men were assisting a wounded man out of the wheat, and I was carrying his rifle, an enemy plane flew right over our heads, didn't seem to be 500 feet high. The gun I was carrying was loaded and had a full magazine so I had the satisfaction of firing two shots at the plane before he zoomed up and away. In firing I remembered my quail and duck wing shooting days in Texas. I led the plane several yards, but if the bullet hit it, no apparent injury was done. It isn't often that colonels and the like get an opportunity to fire a shot in a big battle. A little later a French plane was shot down and swooped, rather than fell, 100 yards from us. It landed without crashing out in no-man's-land in the wheat. A minute or two later the Boche turned a number of machine guns on it. The aviator must have had a great surprise, as I am sure he thought he was landing in the rear of our front lines; I do not know what happened to him.

At 7:15 a.m. and again at 9:32 a.m. I sent written messages to the brigade commander describing conditions. These conditions were, in brief, that the 26th and 28th infantries were stopped on the western edge of the Paris-Soissons road. From our left flank the enemy was delivering an accurate rifle, machine gun and artillery fire, and from slightly higher ground in front (east) of our lines the enemy appeared to be in considerable force and any movement forward was met by heavy machine gun fire. The light artillery barrage had either ceased or long since gone beyond us. I urged that the French or some force be sent up to clear the area to our left, and that the artillery concentrate its fire on the enemy positions about 200 yards east of the Paris-Soissons road. Another report, with a map, was sent to the brigade via the regimental P.C. at Le Mont d'Arly at 2:55 p.m. I also wrote a note to Major Ruggles, giving him as accurately as possible the exact areas on which I wanted him to fire. Nothing happened, and not a word was received from the brigade or the division or the regimental headquarters until about 3:15 p.m., when a messenger from the operations officer, Lieutenant Marshall, notified me that another attack would probably be ordered for 4:00 p.m. in conjunction with the 26th Infantry and the French.

With this warning notice came a map indicating the south and north limits of the 28th Infantry. The northern (left-hand) limit included all the area north of the Breuil-Ploisy road at that moment very much occupied by the enemy. Naturally I assumed that Marshall had received or copied the map from one sent to him from the brigade, in which case it clearly indicated that although I had already explained, in detail, the situation as early as 7:15 a.m. they still knew nothing about it. After the battle Marshall told me that a Captain Johnston of the staff of the French regiment on our left gave him the limits allotted to the 28th Infantry. Conditions at the front, no food, little rest, severe losses, made the command of a regiment no sinecure, and the stupidity of an important staff officer didn't help matters.

It should be remembered that the 28th employed only the remnants of the Second and Third battalions. The First Battalion, still held as division reserve, was commanded by Major George F. Rozelle (W.P. 1903).

I directed Major Huebner to prepare to attack, but not to move forward until I directed him to do so. I sent a message to the brigade, stating that the 28th Infantry could not form up on the ground indicated as the area was fully occupied by the enemy, and that the French regiment had not taken it, as reported by me at 9:32 a.m. Returning to the P.C. in the cave at Le Mont d'Arly, I got the division on the phone and explained, in detail, the exact front line conditions of my regiment. General Summerall directed me to attack from the ground now held by the regiment, that troops would come up on my left. Later, he informed me that this message indicated to him I was prone to see obstacles, that he did not want officers in his division to make reports concerning obstacles in their sector.

As a regimental commander, responsible for the lives of my officers and enlisted men, as well as the operations of the regiment, I thought it necessary, and still think it was my duty, to place all facts before my superiors. They, then, with all the information available, can act intelligently. This was not what General Summerall wanted a regimental commander to do; he wanted no information, just go forward. He liked to talk seriously in preposterously heroic phrases. Once I heard him say that he had visited many battalions that had not gained their objective, but as long as one man remained, there was no excuse. In July, 1918, I did not know the type of man he was.

After my telephone conversation with the division I sent word to Major Rozelle whose battalion had just been released to me to push forward as soon as troops came up on his left. A few moments later the French Captain Johnston came to my P.C. and said the French intended reattacking over the ground not gained in the morning. At 3:15 p.m. the First Battalion followed by the remnants of the Second and Third battalions advanced towards Ploisy.

In addition to the hundreds of prisoners we captured in the caves near Le Mont d'Arly there were hundreds of small arms, individual shoulder packs, horses, a wagon, and a little donkey. The donkey may have been of French extraction but the 28th after the battle kept him for a mascot. I examined several of the shoulder packs carried by the infantry soldier. The contents looked exactly alike and were models of uniformity. The main part of the pack, the knapsack, was made of leather with the hair on it; this helped in shedding rain and snow. Among the many articles carried were two neat piles of clean rectangular rags. One set was packed with a container for gun oil, the other with a box of dubbing (grease) for keeping boot leather soft. In what appeared to be noncommissioned officers' knapsacks were small maps of the Soissons area. These maps were almost as good as the ones furnished regimental commanders by our division; and, unlike my flimsy, easily torn paper map the German maps were cloth backed or printed on cloth.

Late in the afternoon of the nineteenth during the attack on the Ploisy ravine, Major Huebner was wounded. He turned the command of the two battalions over to Second Lieutenant J. J. Parker, N.A., who later received the Congressional Medal of Honor for conspicuous gallantry in carrying his command forward.

Major Huebner is a most distinguished and gallant officer, a courageous leader of combat troops. He was awarded the Distinguished Service Cross for heroic conduct at Cantigny in May, 1918, where his battalion lost half its officers and 30 percent of the enlisted men. He was awarded an oak-leaf cluster on his D.S.C. for great gallantry at the Battle of Soissons. He was also awarded the Distinguished Service Medal for most conspicuous services in the 28th Infantry during the war.

The Congressional Medal reached back for decades but until just before World War I had often been indifferently awarded; the result was a re-examination of the terms of awards and many holders were asked to send back their medals. The second medal for valor was the Distinguished Service Cross, at first a small star on a theater service medal or ribbon. It was extended backward to the Spanish-American War, and many awards were made after World War I, with the result being award of several thousand stars and, in the time of General Douglas MacArthur's service as chief of staff, converted to medals (the chief of staff received seven). The D.S.C. often was awarded for administrative performance, not valor. The Distinguished Service Medal was solely for administrative performance. The Purple Heart, for wounds, at first was a chevron on the holder's blouse, converted to a medal.

About 8:30 p.m., long after dark, and after sanguinary fighting, a mile and a half advance was made to the east edge of the Ploisy ravine. Berzy-le-Sec might have been captured that evening, but the deep dark ravine disorganized the attacking battalion, part of which did reach the outskirts of Berzy and then fell back the 1,200 yards to the Ploisy ravine. Although our divisional training neither required nor advised brigade and regimental commanders to accompany front line battalions in action, and certainly up to that time I know of no regimental commander who had actually led "his" regiment in battle, I am certain that when Ploisy was captured I should have been there. Perhaps I might have had sufficient energy to push on the weary men of the First Battalion and taken Berzy that night. A little of our Civil War medicine is what we lacked in the Great War, and what is still lacking in this World War.

In Ploisy, the front line sheltered themselves behind the steep bank of the ravine and, where the right section of the line had advanced beyond the ravine, the men dug "foxholes" deep enough for protection from the small arm and machine gun bullets flying overhead from Berzy-le-Sec German artillery from north and east of the Farm du Mount de Courmelles, poured a flanking fire into our lines. This was the area allotted for capture to the French; so, again, I lay part of our troubles to a French failure to capture their objective. I am sure they made every effort to do so, and my criticism of their failure may be entirely unjustified.

In passing judgment on the failure of the French and the 2nd Brigade to capture their objective on schedule, it is necessary to remember that more than forty-eight hours had passed since anyone at the front had food or drink. Nothing had yet come from the supply company of the regiment. Even under fire, the men slept in their little shelter holes dug in the hot wheat fields, or near the top of the steep sides of the ravines, a sleep of sheer exhaustion.

In addition to the bloody fighting in the wheat fields, the 2nd Brigade had to force its way through the deep, wide, and defended ravines of Le Mont d'Arly, Missy-aux-Bois, and Ploisy. Another excuse, if one is needed, to defend the great gallantry of this brigade is the fact that the enemy defense of the huge salient, which we of the 10th Army were attempting to reduce, became stiffer and was held more vigorously the nearer one approached the west hinge, six miles west of Soissons, or the east hinge at Rheims some 35 miles southeast of Soissons.

The lower end of this German salient on the eighteenth of July passed through Château-Thierry, 25 miles south of a line between Soissons and

Rheims. As the enemy retired from this deep thrust into the lines of the French Army, the most southern part (vicinity of Château-Thierry) retired faster and farther than elsewhere on the long perimeter of the salient; and as the enemy line approached the hinges above mentioned it held longer, retired more unwillingly, and the fighting was fiercer.

In the First Division the 28th Infantry was nearest the Soissons hinge, and while I do not claim the Germans opposed us more strenuously than they did the French, still nearer Soissons, I do contend that the 2nd Brigade had more opposition and a more difficult terrain to capture than the 1st Brigade to our right, and far more opposition than the Second Division, three or four miles to our right.

General Pershing in his book says, "Although the success of the 1st and 2nd divisions near Soissons on the first two days of the attack had started the withdrawal of the German armies, they fought desperately from position to position and their retirement was skillfully conducted throughout in an effort to save men and material from capture. . . . The French and American troops east of Château-Thierry did not advance immediately. On the 20th, however, patrols from the 3rd Division discovered that the Germans had withdrawn and on the 21st the Division crossed the Marne in pursuit." These paragraphs written by the c.-in-c. Indicate where the toughest fighting took place.

The two infantry brigades within the First Division were numbered 1st and 2nd, and within subsequent divisions the numbers so followed; hence in the Second Division the infantry brigades were 3rd and 4th. Infantry regiments in the First were 16th and 18th in the 1st Brigade, 26th and 28th in the 2nd Brigade; this was because the First Division went over to France initially and the War Department assigned it such infantry regiments from the Regular Army as it could fill easily. Babcock in the above pages was complaining not merely of the division commander, General Summerall, but of the 28th Infantry's brigade commander, Beaumont Buck. In retrospect it would have been possible to contend, about divisional organization in World War I, that the brigades often were superfluous, but for the War Department in 1917 their creation was irresistible, for they offered dozens of promotions for Regular Army colonels.

2

Early in the morning of the twentieth I investigated the situation with Major Rozelle. The 28th held the Mount de Courmelles Farm in liaison with a group of French troops, Ploisy and the western edge of the plateau east of Ploisy in liaison with the 26th Infantry. Due to the peculiar shape of this plateau, the enemy had direct observation on our troops from the northeast of the Courmelles Farm, from Berzy and from higher ground east of that village.

Returning to Missy-aux-Bois, where the telephone line had been extended during the forenoon of the twentieth, I found a rolling kitchen serving hot food to all comers in the ravine. Some of this food had been carried forward to Ploisy.

At 1:15 p.m. I received an order to attack Berzy-le-Sec at 2:00 p.m. This time, 45 minutes, was given to send a messenger or go myself the two miles to Ploisy and to give Major Rozelle an opportunity to put his battalion in motion. The order stated that the barrage would be light and would "mark a line for the troops." Having just come from the front line, knowing how small in numbers and how weary the men were and what great losses had already occurred, I felt it my duty as the regimental commander to make an effort to save some of their lives and get my gallant soldiers some real artillery support. As accurately as conditions permitted, the twelve companies now on or just behind the firing line, on the afternoon of the twentieth of July, consisted of 10 officers and about 300 enlisted men. The remainder of the 2,400 that had started the attack on July 18 were either dead, wounded, or shirking, hiding in the wheat or in the stone houses at Breuil, Missy or Ploisy. To attack Berzy-le-Sec over a flat plain 1,200 yards wide under clear observation by the enemy, with their guns sweeping it from three sides, was sure to cause further heavy casualties unless we were given strong artillery support.

So I spoke to General Buck over the telephone in words well remembered, and later written down by me, due to my desperate attempts to get the brigade and through the brigade the division to realize the situation at the firing front. I said, "General, I do not wish to appear as a kicker, but as regimental commander I believe we ought to have more artillery support, especially on the guns of the enemy north of us and east of Berzy-le-Sec. I believe we will sustain more heavy losses if we attack as ordered."

General Buck replied, 'That is all right, Colonel. It is your duty (or right) to report these matters," or words to that effect. When this conversation was reported to General Summerall, he noted it against me.

The attack arrangements were not altered. I went, at once, by motorcycle side car to Ploisy to arrange for the attack. I found Rozelle in his dugout. He said an order had come to him to attack at 1:00 p.m. and that Lieutenant S. C. Sorenson with two companies was making the attack. I read the order and was of the opinion that it was merely a warning order sent to him by the brigade. Major Rozelle from his dugout in the Ploisy ravine really didn't know whether Sorenson was attacking or not. In fact due to exhaustion, this battalion commander appeared mentally well below par.

The warning order did suggest that we use the infiltration method of attacking, so I seized upon that as offering a much better chance of success, without the heavy losses sure to follow a frontal afternoon attack over that projectile swept plateau without strong artillery support.

I ordered Rozelle to get out and, at once, organize three or four small groups (two squads each) and under the 2:00 p.m. barrage to filter these groups into Berzy by passing along the tree bordered Ploisy ravine and entering Berzy from the north side of that village. This done, to send over more troops until he had his small battalion in Berzy-le-Sec. The attempt was made by Sorenson, a courageous, energetic officer, and he and his groups reached the outskirts of Berzy; but heavy enemy machine gun fire made it impossible, in Sorenson's opinion, to enter the village until after dark.

Returning to the telephone, which had been brought forward to Ploisy, I reported what had been accomplished and notified General Buck that we would capture Berzy-le-Sec during the night. A company was directed to reinforce Sorenson at midnight.

At 11:00 p.m. I was notified that an intense bombardment would fall on the town of Berzy-le-Sec at 4:45 a.m., July 21. Clearly, when that notice arrived, a notice that showed there was absolutely no coordination between the division and its attacking elements, no reliance could be made on what the brigade had but just authorized me to do; either the brigade failed to notify the division as to what the 28th Infantry intended doing that night, or the division completely ignored the brigade. In either case, there I was with a few of my men near Berzy, a large group about to leave, and a heavy barrage designated to fall on them and the village in the early morning. Instead of saving some of the lives of my men, my plan, had it gone through, might have caused further heavy loss.

Personally routing out Rozelle, the company movement was stopped just in time, and a message was sent to Sorenson's groups to fall back. Later that night of July 20–21, the division ordered the 2nd Brigade to attack at 8:30 a.m., July 21. This is the only full daylight morning?? attack I ever heard of or ever participated in during my army career.

My P. C. was in Ploisy, less than one hundred yards behind the front line. At 7:00 a.m., July 21, I consulted with Major Rozelle and spoke to the men lying in their little foxholes along the front line. It was a beautiful morning and not a shot was being fired from either side.

The artillery barrage was scheduled for 8:30 a.m., but at that hour not a sound of firing came from our rear, not a projectile was heard passing overhead. The attacking line rose from their shelter trenches and advanced towards Berzy. Immediately the crash of bursting shells and the swish of small arms bullets made their presence known all along the line. At 8:40 a.m. a few friendly shells were heard passing on their journey to the enemy, but it was a misnomer to call such artillery support a barrage. It may have been one six gun battery firing. Just as Rozelle and the last wave of his little force climbed out of the Ploisy ravine, someone notified me that General Buck was near at hand. I found him with one or two of his staff officers and Sorenson (who had received a bullet through his body) seated in an enlarged foxhole on the plateau east of the ravine. Sorenson recovered from his wound, only to die in Germany, after the Armistice, in a motor car accident.

With about 20 percent casualties, the town of Berzy-le-Sec was captured at 9:15 a.m. and an hour later the railroad embankment and road in the bottom of the Berzy ravine was taken by the regiment. By motorcycle side car I followed the regiment to the town, and from the top of one of the stone buildings there could see Soissons and the movement of people and transport vehicles on the streets through my field glasses. To the east the ravine or broad valley extended to Noyant-et-Aconin built on the steep east side, where the enemy had retired. Both sides of this picturesque valley were covered with trees.

Returning to Ploisy, I telephoned the division chief of staff, Colonel Campbell King (now a retired major general), that the 28th had Berzy-le-Sec and the front lines were along the railroad track in the bottom of the valley, some 1,000 yards to the east. King was warm in his congratulations.

During the five days in the front line there were several incidents, gruesome or exciting, that may interest readers of these chronicles. On the afternoon of July 19, just as I left the Missy-aux-le-Bois ravine to walk back to the front on the rock and sand road between that village and the Paris-Soissons road, a French infantry regiment north of the road was observed moving forward in "artillery columns" formation. The blue gray uniformed men were in widely separated groups of tightly closed files. They were about 200 yards to my left and abreast of me, then suddenly the enemy artillery opened on them with what appeared to be shells of at least 155-mm. caliber. It was appalling to see the little groups run forward, then stop and crouch down, each man snuggling up to the man in front of him as if the touch of his battle pack gave protection and courage. The big shells sank into the heavy soil and then exploded, sending great geysers of dirt fifty feet high. Occasionally I heard cries and shouts from the regiment, but it went forward, the shells shortening their range as the men advanced. Fortunately the ground being soft there were no shell fragments, so I imagine that except where a shell fell on one of the little human clusters the casualties were nil. It was a veritable moving picture to me. There I was within 200 yards of a regiment under heavy and terrifying artillery shelling and as safe as if I was seeing it on the screen. Where I was the road was hard, and not being certain that some gunner might accidentally or on purpose divert a shell in my direction, I moved a hundred yards south of the road to nice soft ground and resumed my walk in perfect safety.

The individual foxholes dug in the heavy soil east of Ploisy ravine retained many of their excavators by the morning of the twenty-first of July. Returning from the village of Berzy that afternoon, I passed a foxhole that to me was the personification of sheer horror. Kneeling in the shallow trench was a dead man. From his hobnailed shoes to the top of his olive drab infantry breeches he was fully clothed. From the waist to his neck, he had been stripped by something that, on the ghastly white flesh, had left a few small black marks. Of his rifle, belt, gas mask, battle pack, coat, shirt, undershirt there wasn't a sign. His hair, eyebrows and eyelashes were gone, and the entire top of his head had disappeared taking with it all that one is supposed to have in the skull. Grim and hardened to suffering and frightfulness as the past four days had made me, this last horror made my very soul shudder. Probably, although I am only guessing, this soldier was the victim of a high explosive shell that burst just as it tipped the top of his head or helmet. The blast removed his equipment and clothing, removed the top of his skull with more than expert surgical ability. The whole operation left him still kneeling, facing the enemy.

During the morning hours of the twenty-second of July, I visited Major Rozelle and his little command in Berzy-le-Sec, and arranged for his relief that evening by a battalion of Scots. It was a hot sunny day, and not having arranged to be met by motorcycle side cars for myself and runner, I decided to shorten the return trip by walking across the open plain to Ploisy. Directing the runner to keep 100 yards behind me so that if we were fired upon the same shell couldn't get us both, we started. We were three or four hundred yards west of Berzy when an enemy 77-mm. shell hit hard ground and burst one or two hundred yards in front of me. This did not worry me as I thought it might have been a shell either falling well beyond Berzy or very short of Ploisy. I had no idea the German artillery would waste ammunition on two men. About a minute later another shell fell behind me and not far from my runner. I knew that sign well. Some battery had bracketed us, and the next shell, splitting the ranges of the first two, might be a bull's-eye. Quickly adopting the zigzag method of going forward, so well illustrated then and again now by ocean vessels, we took up the double-time and ran diagonally off to our right. Evidently some enemy artillery gunner had his field glasses well focused on us, his third shell followed our right-hand deviation but hit the ground between us, throwing up a tall column of dirt. Dropping to the ground or in any old shell hole near at hand, we recovered our wind and then again trotted off on our devious line towards safety and the Ploisy ravine.

I am sure the enemy gunner and his crew enjoyed chasing us across that long hot site of nine hundred yards of open country. They might be considered first class artillery marksmen, I suppose, but although they at times didn't miss either of us over fifty feet it wasn't close enough for high explosive shell falling in heavy soil. Had they used shrapnel it certainly would have been another story. Only in that case I should have remained on the ground until the enemy grew tired of firing or were sure they had done for us; and in all probability they would have. Finally we both reached the edge of the Ploisy ravine, and descending a few yards I turned to the right and the runner and I seated ourselves under a tree. While congratulating each other on our luck we endeavored to wipe off the sweat and dirt of our cross country run.

In coming down from the plateau into the ravine I noticed a soldier sitting in a shallow hole, or niche, dug into the side of the bank two or three feet down from the top. These holes had been part of the First Battalion front line of the morning before, and were now very thinly held by the survivors of the Second and Third battalions, acting as regimental reserve. The runner and I hadn't been seated more than a minute when a shell hit the bank exactly where I had descended, buried itself and burst with a roar and another geyser of dirt. At the same time the top of the ravine for several yards slid down the bank. Rising quickly I said to the runner that the Boche still seemed to be after us, and we better move on. As I spoke I happened to look back towards the spot where the shell had burst and saw a hand sticking up among the top lumps of rolling dirt. Then I remembered the soldier in the foxhole, now buried alive—one of the most dreaded battle deaths imaginable. Running back the few yards that separated us I seized his moving fingers and immediately his hand relaxed. Using the edge of my steel hat as a shovel I worked desperately removing the dirt down his arm, at the same time sending the runner along the old line for a small entrenching shovel or anything to dig with. In what may not have been over a minute but to me seemed hours I dug the soft earth away from his arm and upper chest. At that point my hat shovel struck metal; discarding the hat, I scraped about with my fingers and got my thumbs under the brim of a steel helmet. As I raised the brim I had a terrible feeling that I might see a badly lacerated face or head or the face of a smothered man. What I saw was the grin of an unshaven, dirty faced American young man; before I could say a word he looked me in the eye and said, as cool as a cucumber, "I'm all right, colonel." My relief was so great I almost laughed, and I replied, "Well, you are the pluckiest damn man I ever saw; where in hell are your legs?" With his free arm, he pointed in their direction and the runner having returned with a shovel soon dug this fine young 28th infantryman out of a twenty-two inch deep grave.

His life was saved by pure luck, coupled with one fortunate circumstance. As the shell exploded he was sitting in the hole with his back to the ravine. As the landslide rolled over him, it tipped his steel helmet over his face. This kept dirt out of his nose and mouth and there was a hat full of air held right where it was needed. He must have raised one arm, perhaps to grab his hat, but the mass of dirt caught it and buried it to his wrist a full arm's length above the shoulder leaving the twitching fingers for me to luckily see. When most of the dirt had been removed he lifted himself and sitting on the edge of his late tomb proceeded to dig earth out of his neck, hair, and ears. I took him with me to the P.C., not far away, and told him to take the day off, that he had had his share of the war for that day. Why I didn't write down his name and company I don't know, perhaps finding two Scottish officers waiting to see me caused this neglect. I would give a great deal to know if my fine young soldier survived the war.

As I entered the little French cottage where the regimental P.C. then was, I was introduced to two handsome, immaculate looking young lieutenants from an infantry battalion of the 15th Scottish Division. These fresh, pink cheeked lads shook my grimy hand and, from their look of surprise, apparently thought that even for an American regimental commander I was a sad looking one. Covered with dirt, soaking wet with sweat, I must have been a great contrast to their battalion commander who had sent them up to find out from me what the front line conditions were, as well as for them to make a personal reconnaissance of our front line. After a brief description as to where our front line was and how it was being held, these officers were supplied with a guide, and with a recommendation that they do some zigzagging should they travel over the plateau to Berzy. Off they went, two highly polished, almost pretty kid "left-tenants." Two or three hours later, two sweaty, dirty, out of breath young men returned. They gave me a rather more appreciative look, thanked us for the guide and information. In leaving, one lad remarked, "I say, you know, sir; that is a hell of a place, sir."

Several thousand yards away to the east I am sure a squad of German artillerymen were still laughing over the kilted figures that had run, risen, run and risen on their circuitous course over the grass covered Berzy-le-Sec—Ploisy plateau.

Under a cloudless sky, the country bathed in full moonlight, I watched the platoons of the Scots as they marched briskly forward out of the Ploisy ravine on the road to Berzy-le-Sec the evening of the twenty-second of July. Led by an upstanding young officer, each platoon many of them pitifully small in numbers passed in perfect formation, a sergeant and two litter bearers bringing up the rear. Three or four hours later we heard the thunder of the guns heralding their attack: their losses were severe and I fear many of the casualties were beyond the need of a litter bearer.

By 2:00 a.m. on the twenty-third of July, what was left of the 28th Infantry, some 1,300 or 1,400 officers and enlisted men (including all the rear elements—a big supply company of about 160 men, a headquarters company of over 300 men, and the slackers were bivouacked in the Forêt de Villers-Cotterets. My Dodge automobile picked up several of us in the Ploisy ravine and took us to this rendezvous, and as we arrived a messenger or mail orderly from the headquarters company brought me a bundle of mail; and, "believe it or not", the first envelope opened directed me to send to one of the corps schools several captains and lieutenants, twelve or fifteen officers as I now remember. Imagine a training system that contemplated training officers who had just completed five days of most exacting and practical combat fighting, at a corps school where the instructors were totally ignorant of real fighting. In my half-starved exhausted condition I think I tore that order to pieces.

So after an almost continuous advance for 3½ days, and losses unsurpassed by any American division before or since, the 28th Infantry completed its more than five mile backward sweep of the enemy line; and two weeks later I was relieved from command of this fine regiment at General Summerall's request, because as he explained to me he took exception to my telephone calls to him on the nineteenth and to General Buck on the twentieth.

Long after dark on the nineteenth of July, General Summerall came to the regimental P.C. in the Missy-aux-Bois ravine and criticized my reporting to him that the French had not taken their objectives for the day and in consequence my regiment could not form up on the ground directed. He threatened to relieve me then.

On August 2, 1918, in the course of a private conversation with him in his office, he informed me that he had no fault to find with my personal courage or bearing in the presence of the enemy, that he considered me "an accomplished officer"; that he had no fault to find with my handling of the 28th Infantry in the battle; that the regiment had done well (he should have said magnificently); but that he considered me so constituted that I was prone to see obstacles in my path when executing military duties. That he would not have in his division any officer who even thought an order of his was not capable of complete fulfillment. That he had no time to listen to reports from anyone about military situations in front of attacking troops that would prevent his orders from being strictly carried out. That he knew all about the difficulties, didn't wish to be told about them. That he was prepared to sacrifice the entire division if he thought best to carry out his orders (I can well believe that) and that all he wanted was for us all to simply go forward regardless of conditions.

And that is what his admirers would call the characteristics of a leader. Summerall is a completely ruthless driver of men; has a fine voice, an excellent command of heroic phrases and a complete ignorance as to infantry fighting, how to fight that branch of the service.

Babcock never learned of a letter that passed between two prominent major generals of the AEF in 1927, concerning the death of his fellow infantry commander in the 2nd Brigade, Colonel Hamilton Smith (26th Regiment), involving General Summerall:

"Last Sunday morning I was at Walter Reed Hospital looking over construction, and saw Major Kenner at a distance. I called him over to ask if you had seen him while you were here and he said you had not. I told him that you wanted to know about the death of Colonel Hamilton Smith and he told me all about it. He drew a map in the sand giving me the approximate location of the Twenty-sixth and Sixteenth Infantry at the time in question, and then showed me exactly how Colonel Smith went over into the German lines and was killed. I have tried to describe this in a rough way on a piece of paper.

"Major Kenner knew all about the interview Colonel Smith had. He was with Colonel Smith at that time, but was standing off at a distance. A short time after that the Commanding General of the First Division came along and Kenner was so close that he heard the entire conversation. The Commanding General asked Colonel Smith where his front was located. Colonel Smith took out his map and described in detail where the troops were. He then asked him if he had been up there personally to see if this was correct, and Colonel Smith said no, that he just had the word from his liaison officer Lieutenant Holmes. The Commanding General expressed surprise that he had not been there himself and asked in a perfectly brutal way if he was afraid to go, and with that statement left him.

"Immediately after this Colonel Smith went up to his front line. When he got to the front line he dismissed his orderly and went right straight on over in front of his troops. Just in front of the Twenty-sixth Infantry there was a cut through which a railroad ran. He went down over that and came up on the other bank. A short distance in front of this bank was a ravine which he went through and came up in an open field right in front of the Germans. The Germans saw him all the time and could have killed him at any time, but they allowed him to go along until he got into a little cluster of woods. Just what happened there nobody knows, but the Boche delivered one volley from their machine gun located in the place I have tried to indicate.

"Kenner was up at the front with the troops and they were perfectly sure that Colonel Smith had been shot and Kenner desired to go across at once but they said that that would be suicide. However after looking the situation over for a while he made a quick run for the cut through which the railroad passed. This was done so quickly that the Boche did not get him, although they fired a volley at him too late. He then went on all fours to the right through this cut, kept low down on all fours or lower, and went over to the ravine. He then went up the ravine until he was about opposite the place he thought Colonel Smith was in the woods, and then went through the grass, protected by the woods from the view of the Boche, and located Colonel Smith.

"Smith was still living when Kenner got to him. He tried to speak but he could not. Kenner remained with Colonel Smith until dark when a patrol came into No Man's Land and they all carried Colonel Smith back to their own regiment. Colonel Smith went over toward the Germans about five o'clock in the afternoon. Kenner says it was a perfectly straight case of suicide on Colonel Smith's part. He says that he thinks that he was mentally upset by his interview with the Commanding General and thought he would rather pursue his course than to face any remarks the Commanding General might make with reference to him.

"Kenner was evidently devoted to Colonel Smith. He thought he was one of the finest characters that he ever knew and spoke of him as a perfectly splendid soldier. There was a Lieutenant Leggs, who is still in the service, who, I think, was present at the interview between Colonel Smith and the Commanding General."

"Kenner said he would send me the French map that he had in his possession that date, but when he went to look among his papers he could not locate it. The rough sketch I have made on paper is perfectly clear in my mind from the marks Major Kenner made on the sand last Sunday. So there is the story from Kenner, who probably knew more about Smith's death than any other man." (Merritte W. Ireland to John L. Hines, July 1, 1927, box 28, Hines papers, U.S. Army Military History Institute, Army War College, Carlisle Barracks, Pennsylvania.)

Major General Ireland had been surgeon general of the AEF and currently was surgeon general of the War Department. Hines had been commanding general of the Fourth Division and of the III Corps during the war, had just retired as chief of staff in the War Department and currently was commander of the Ninth Corps Area, a postwar administrative district with headquarters in San Francisco; he had succeeded General Pershing as chief of staff and was followed by General Summerall.

Seven

Tactics

On August 5, Colonel G. C. Barnhardt (W.P. 1892), a classmate of General Summerall's, came to my headquarters and relieved me from the command of my fine regiment. It was a bitter blow.

In the division telegram asking that I be relieved, it was recommended that I be transferred to another division. Fortunately for me, a good friend and classmate of mine, Brigadier General Robert C. Davis, was the adjutant general of the AEF. Writing him a long letter explaining the events that culminated in my relief from command, I asked him to get me another regimental command: that, if necessary, I was prepared to ask for a court of inquiry in order to prove every word of the statements I had written him. This letter I sent by motorcycle messenger to Chaumont. Almost immediately a telegram came ordering me to the Eighty-ninth Division. A real friend is a jewel without price.

1

Headquarters of the Eighty-ninth Division was at Lagney in the province of Meurthe et Moselle four miles north of Toul when I reported on August 7, 1918, but moved to Lucey, a mile south, a few days later. The division commander was Brigadier General Frank L. Winn (W.P. 1886). Colonel James E. Reeves (W.P. 1892) was the assigned commanding officer of the 353rd Infantry but, at this time, was in temporary command of the 177th Infantry Brigade while the assigned commander of that brigade

(Winn) was commanding the division. I was assigned as temporary commander of Reeves's regiment.

The Eighty-ninth Division, one of the new National Army divisions, had been organized and trained at Camp Funston near Fort Riley, Kansas, under Major General Leonard Wood, from September, 1917, to June, 1918. By the middle of June, the Eighty-ninth was in camp near the cathedral city of Winchester, England. A few days later the division reached France via Cherbourg and Le Havre. Thereafter the division went through the training curriculum.

Camps and their metropolitan equivalents, forts, were named after deceased officers; Major General Funston, the former colonel of the 20th Nebraska National Guard Regiment, promoted to general because of his capture of Aguinaldo, died in February, 1917.

Each infantry company was equipped with 16 French Chauchat automatic rifles, machine gun companies with 16 Vickers guns each; hobnailed field shoes replaced the garrison russet shoe, the little overseas cap and steel helmet the felt campaign hat, and the gas mask became almost as much a part of the uniform as the blouse; wrapped cloth leggings were substituted for the canvas leggings. The blouse, worn by all officers and soldiers at this time, had a standing collar about an inch high, closed at the neck with two hook and eye fasteners and buttoned down the front with five dark (bronze, so called) buttons, also four outside bronze buttoned pockets. The dismounted breeches were worn, and the olive drab colored flannel shirt. In the trenches or when going into action, officers no longer wore the leather Sam Browne belt, which had proved itself to be a dangerously distinguishing mark. All officers, up to and including battalion commanders, carried the rifle. Neither of these simple devices to reduce casualties was in force in the First Division up to the time I left. At Soissons all officers wore the Sam Browne belt either with one or two leather cross belts and no rifles were carried. Well do I remember the pathetic sight of a tall slim kid second lieutenant lying dead near the narrow path in the Missy-aux-Bois ravine, his face covered with a handkerchief, his brand new light leather Sam Browne belt, possibly the target that drew the enemy bullet, buckled snugly around his waist and right shoulder.

The belt was a requirement of General Pershing for all officers in the AEF, to distinguish them from officers in the United States. Browne was an officer of the British Indian Army who invented the belt to distinguish an officer, assist with averdupois, and hang equipment of sorts. The wartime U.S. Army chief of staff in the War Department in Washington, General Peyton C. March, considered the belt an affectation and forbade its wearing in the United States.

The 353rd Infantry was a well organized, well disciplined regiment. I had never seen a more intelligent and finer appearing lot of officers and men. The regiment was almost at full war strength (3,806) and had a splendid band. The enlisted men had been drafted from the Middle West, Kansas and Nebraska. The officers came very largely from the Colorado Officers Training Camp.

One battalion of my new regiment was in the front line about one kilometer north of the Pont-à-Mouson-St. Mihiel road, the support battalion some three kilometers south of that road in an entrenched position called the position of resistance, and the reserve battalion was back in Manorville.

Every day or two I made a thorough tour of the front line system of trenches. The little village of Limey, completely evacuated by civilians, was just a mass of stone ruins. It is on the Pont-à-Mousson road and was in the sector of the 353rd Infantry. From the village and the road in our sector a series of deep connecting trenches extended up to the trench system of the front line. The St. Mihiel salient had been fought over and occupied by the French and Germans since 1914. Each army had captured and occupied portions of their enemy's trench system, then lost them, then recaptured them, each time converting them to their defense needs. As a result the entire area was a mass of ditches, dugouts and wire, a labyrinthean system of ditches where it was easy to get lost until one climbed out and surveyed the area from the ground surface.

No attempt was made to occupy the entire firing line of the front line system. Instead platoons occupied certain sections where they had a clear field of rifle, automatic and machine gun fire to the right and left covering the area in front of the trench system leading to the nearest platoon to their right and left. The company support to the front line platoon or platoons was located in one or two places in a trench, a hundred or two hundred yards to the rear, having a good approach trench leading up to the front line platoon it was supporting. After dark, carrying parties went back about 2 ½ miles to the vicinity of the position in headquarters where the supply company kitchens had set up, by animal-drawn transport from near Manonville, the marmite cans of hot food and coffee for the next three meals. All this went on just ten miles north of the fortress city of Toul and its 13,000 inhabitants.

With the lessons of the Battle of Soissons fresh in my mind I decided to pass them on to this big inexperienced National Army regiment and at the same time instruct them in a combat formation which I had devolved from conversations with lieutenants, noncommissioned officers, and privates of the 28th Infantry, many of whom had been recommended for the Distinguished Service Cross.

The need of the New Army was to learn the tactics of European armies, primarily the German Army, in regard to machine guns, artillery, and poison gas. The lessons of Soissons were of the first two, and Babcock learned the third with the Eighty-ninth Division. The initial lesson of Soissons was about machine guns. Generals Pershing and Summerall knew nothing about how to take them, except by rushes, which was near madness against the guns' mechanical efficiency. Pershing, like Babcock, was a cavalryman; Summerall was an artilleryman. Old Army officers, even artillerymen, knew little about European, especially German, artillery tactics. Summerall sensed the need for far more artillery support for the infantry than American artillery tactics required; he was a member of the Baker Board and made this point, at that time to no avail. At Soissons he was not in the front line and like many subsequent artillery brigadiers observing the several casualties of their artillery brigades did not appreciate what infantry casualties could be. The third tactical confusion of American generals was in regard to poison gas, of which Summerall understood nothing. When he took the First Division into the Meuse-Argonne on October 1, 1918, he put infantrymen into several large ravines prior to sending the regiments forward; the gas officers of the German Army knew the location of those ravines and filled them with gas between October 1 and the First Division's time of attack, October 4; the division lost 1,400 men.

From a tactical point of view it was very instructive to learn exactly how small groups of three or four men had actually captured German machine gun nests or pits in the wheat fields. In every case, and many were investigated, the method was essentially the same, and came about as follows:

As the tightly closed up skirmish lines and "artillery column" groups advanced against the enemy in the Battle of Soissons, the accurate and continuous rifle and machine gun fire killed many men, wounded others and caused the less courageous to gather near the bolder spirits, natural battle leaders, or to hide in shell holes or in the thick growing wheat. Very soon the front ground gaining groups were under the command and leadership of the most courageous members of the front line troops. Perhaps these leaders were noncommissioned officers, perhaps inexperienced privates, but in all cases brave men by their display of boldness and ability who became the actual fighting leaders.

It was the fire of the enemy that caused this formation, so I decided that the best formation for attacking troops to adopt was one that battle experience and extreme danger had shown to be the one that they would be "shot into" in action: that was the formation of small combat groups. The method adopted by the natural leaders in overcoming resistance in their front or capturing enemy machine gunners, regardless of the size of the attacking group, was the same. As soon as a group of three or four men came under the fire of an automatic rifleman or machine gunner, the group commander had them lie down or get behind what cover was near at hand. Then, when he thought he knew the approximate position of the enemy strong point, he sent out two flanking groups (perhaps of only one man each) to the right and left to secure a flanking fire on the enemy. As the two groups ran, or crept, or crawled forth on their mission, the remaining men opened up a hot fire on the enemy, hoping to engage his attention and prevent his concentrating on either flanking group.

After a while, one or both of the flanking groups would secure a position from which their rifle or rifle grenade fire would become effective; the enemy, under the combined fire of the three little groups, would surrender or retreat.

Using the three group combat formation as the basic principle of the attack formation, I devised the following formation for the attack by an infantry regiment of the 1918 organization. The "point" or center group, under a noncommissioned officer, consisted of an automatic rifleman, an automatic rifle ammunition carrier, and a rifle grenadier who had a tromblon for firing grenades. The tromblon was a cup shaped device that could be attached to the muzzle of the Springfield rifle, and in this a rifle grenade was placed. When the rifle was fired, the bullet passed through a tunnel extending the length of the grenade while the force of the rifle cartridge explosion shot the grenade fifty yards to the right and left of the point, and about 25 yards less advanced were the two flanking groups, organized as described for the point or center group.

Fifty yards behind the point came the remaining members of the combat group under a sergeant. The other half of the platoon was organized and formed as just described, and either followed the rear element of the leading group by 100 yards or advanced abreast of it, with its interior flanking group at least 75 yards from the flankers of the combat group to the right or left. The officer in command of the platoon then had his two combat groups either on a 175 yard front by 240 yards in depth area or on a 350 yard front by 70 yards in depth.

About 225 yards in rear of the firing platoon came the remaining two platoons of the same company. These platoons advanced in line of combat groups on a front of 350 yards, separated laterally by some 75 yards. Each combat group, under its own leader, advanced in two separate files. The leaders of each little group, having been already designated as point, flankers or support, were able to form the "diamond attack formation" instantly.

At least 200 yards in rear of these platoons came another company with two platoons leading on a front of 350 yards: 150 yards farther to the rear followed the remaining two platoons of this second company. It advanced on the same front all four platoons being formed in what was known as artillery columns. This was a formation in which the big infantry platoons marched in line of squad columns, each squad in column of files.

If the front line battalion was attacking with two companies on the firing line, the two remaining companies formed in the same manner to the right or left of the first two. This put the battalion on a 700 yard front and about 675 yards in depth.

This description of my infantry attack formation may seem a bit involved to the lay mind but actually once the platoons learned the combat group formation and were able to take it up rapidly from any previous formation, the whole regimental attack became very simple.

The formation was designed to give the company commanders, the lieutenants and noncommissioned officers a chance to use their initiative and room in which to exercise it. In the diamond attack formation the little flanking groups had a lateral area of about 125 yards in which they could maneuver, take advantage of any cover in the area, attack in any formation their noncommissioned officer might decide was best. They had just one objective, to assist the advance of the point group. The point group was trained to stay on the prescribed line of advance. They, being the guide of the combat group, kept it in its own combat area which prevented interference with groups to the right and left.

The lesson learned at Soissons, under enemy fire, to keep the enemy machine gun nest or strong point under steady fire while flankers worked around or behind it, was thus accomplished by the point and the two flanking groups of each combat group.

The little reserve, directly led by the sergeant, was available to add to or replace the point or flankers, and, of course, took part in the combat whenever possible from their rear position by firing through the intervals between the point and flankers.

On September 6, Major General William M. Wright (W.P. 1885) assumed command of the division and Brigadier General Winn rejoined the 177th Brigade and Colonel Reeves came back to his regiment, the 353rd Infantry. So, once more, I had lost the command of a fine regiment after a month of most satisfactory service. I fully expected to be retained as second in command to Reeves, but the next day, to my surprise and great satisfaction, I was transferred to the 354th Infantry in the same brigade as the commanding officer. Outwardly the 354th Infantry did not appear to be as smart a regiment as the 353rd; but that didn't worry me. The main thing was to have command of a big infantry regiment.

2

On August 10, 1918, the formation of the First American Army was formally announced. Its sector began at Port-sur-Seille (four miles east of Pont-à-Mousson) thence west to St. Mihiel and north to a point opposite Verdun. The First, Forty-second (Rainbow), and Eighty-ninth divisions formed the IV Corps, commanded by Major General Joseph T. Dickman (W.P. 1881). The I Corps consisted of the Second, Ninetieth, and Eighty-second divisions, commanded by Major General Hunter Liggett (W.P.1879), were to our right and II French Colonial Corps to the left.

By the end of August, 1918, the U.S. First Army was preparing to attack the German salient of St. Mihiel on September 12, and the operation came off as planned, although the Allied commander-in-chief, Marshal Foch, persuaded General Pershing to limit the operation to the salient, not to go forward as U.S. Army planners long had hoped for, to attack the German fortress of Metz and on farther north, if they could, into the Saar basin. The battle did give Pershing's troops tactical experience and, if nothing else, occupied German troops while Foch followed his favorite tactic of pushing them elsewhere.

St. Mihiel offered two dangers for the Americans. For one, it was likely to make them overconfident of their military abilities, as by September 12 the German foe was preparing for a withdrawal and their artillery was partly on the roads north, also the odds between the forces were tremendously in favor of the attackers: the Germans only had 25,000 men in the salient, the Americans attacked with 225,000. Secondly, Foch and Pershing on August 30—September 2 agreed that the Americans after St. Mihiel would attack in the area between the Argonne Forest and the Meuse within two weeks, and this created huge logistical problems as the distance, with poor roads, was fifty miles.

In the IV Corps the attack orders required the Eighty-ninth Division, which had been occupying front line trenches for more than a month, to advance from their positions, while the First and Second divisions had been in a rest area and only took their attack positions a day or two before the twelfth of September. The division orders placed the 178th Brigade (355th and 356th regiments) and the 353rd Regiment in the "jump off" position. One battalion of the 354th was designated as the brigade reserve of the 177th Brigade, the other two battalions as division reserve.

The Eighty-ninth Division was ordered to advance in the direction of Thiaucourt-Dampvitoux with the Forty-second Division on its left and the Second Division of the I Corps on the right. For the attack the front occupied by the advance elements of the Eighty-ninth Division was contracted from ten miles to approximately two and a half miles. It extended from a kilometer north and west of Flirey to the west edge of Limey. The First Battalion moved to this vicinity during the evening of the eleventh of September. The terrain to be attacked was difficult. In our front were the Bois de Mort-Mare and the Bois d'Euvezin, heavy woods, and before reaching them several hundred yards of ground covered with a perfect labyrinth of trenches and thousands of miles of barbed wire. The forest of Mort-Mare was described in the army "estimate of the situation" as the key to the German position between St. Mihiel and Pont-à-Mousson.

IV Corps orders directed the Eighty-ninth Division to make its main or strongest effort on its left in order to assist the Forty-second Division. So Brigadier General Winn, then in command of the division, drew up the division order which placed the entire 178th Brigade commanded by Brigadier General Thomas G. Hanson (W.P.1887) on a front approximately half as wide as that assigned to the other brigade, then commanded by Colonel Reeves, and from the 177th Brigade was taken the division reserve.

The artillery supporting the division consisted of the 55th F.A. Brigade, two regiments of 75's and one regiment of 155 howitzers, under the command of Brigadier General J. A. Shipton (W.P. 1892); also two regiments and two battalions of French field artillery, the 250th, 212th, and 160th, and three trench mortar batteries, the 105th and 108th U.S. and the 176th French. In addition there was some army and corps artillery of large caliber.

The artillery barrage began at 1:00 a.m. September 12 and lasted until 5:00 a.m. when the infantry "went over the top" following the rolling barrage. The enemy was caught in the act of retiring from the salient, and while rearguard elements put up a determined resistance the fighting was not as severe as expected.

The 354th played a very unimportant part in the day's proceedings. September 11–12 in their trenches and then followed the 353rd as brigade support. My advanced headquarters and the remainder of the regiment moved up to a number of dugouts, called gas hollow, about 1,000 yards south of Flirey where we spent the night. Beginning at 1:00 a.m. and for the next four hours the noise was terrific. The roar of those thousands of shells passing over our heads was appalling and one could even feel a morsel of pity for the poor wretches at the receiving end.

We were prepared for an enemy fire of retaliation, both of gas and high explosive, but only a few shots were fired at us, wounding some machine gunners in the division reserve. Shortly after 5:00 a.m. the first prisoners began to go past, but we remained inactive. About 10:30 a.m. I was ordered to send the Third Battalion forward as additional brigade reserve. About noon General Wright directed me to go forward and have some of my companies assist the artillery to pass over the roads that led over what had been no-man's-land. I rode forward and it was a great sight to see the miles of wire and the elaborate trenches the enemy had given up. Little did I think at the time that almost to a day two years later Marion, the boys and myself would motor up to the German front line north of Flirey, that the wire would have disappeared, most of the miles of trenches been filled and that nature would have quite successfully covered the shell pocked ground with a green covering of grass and weeds. The four-hour bombardment and the rolling barrage had shot up the country in great shape, and there were many signs showing how hasty had been the retreat of the enemy. Overturned wagons, all types of equipment, horses already saddled, animals hitched to vehicles all left by the road or scattered over the area. In no-man's-land north of Flirey engineer troops and infantrymen were endeavoring to fill trenches and shell holes, roll up wire, and cut a road passage through the trench parapets.

The night before had been cold and rainy and the country road through the forest of Mort-Mare and to the north was very bad. About 4:00 p.m. the regiment reached the outskirts of the village of Euvezin, where we remained until after dark. One or two scouting enemy planes had been flying over the area, and I had the battalion commander march his command up the side of a high prehistoric river bank that faced south; this gave the men almost perfect protection from any long range artillery firing that the enemy might at that hour been in a position to deliver. Nothing however happened. To the best of my recollection we had had a hot breakfast and dinner before leaving gas hollow, so with what food each individual carried we were far better off than the two battalions backing up the 353rd Infantry.

After dark I was ordered to move forward, assemble my regiment and report to General Winn. Up to that time I had been riding, but in order to set the pace for the dismounted headquarters group as well as the Second Battalion, I walked. The night was clear and very dark and the horizon to the north and west of us was aflame with the reflection of many fires and the air trembled with the concussion of the exploding shells as the Germans destroyed their ammunition dumps. It was a really awe inspiring sight. About 9:00 p.m. we arrived at Bouillonville and were joined by the First and Third battalions. Here we slept on the ground in a cold wind under a broken railroad bridge. About 2:00 a.m. I got to sleep for an hour and a half as I was very busy trying to find the brigade commander and getting my regiment so coordinated that we could move forward the next morning.

Early in the morning of the thirteenth of September, as the First Battalion was deploying just north of Bouillonville to begin the advance, an enemy observation plane flew toward us. It wasn't 200 feet high. Glancing up I saw the German Maltese cross on the wings, could see the pilot distinctly. Not a shot had been fired at him by us. I called out, "Fire at that airplane" and as he circled over us the whole battalion began firing. If any bullets hit the plane they didn't bring it down, but the pilot put his ship into a steep climb and was soon far away.

The First Battalion, Major Thomas S. Bridges (W.P. 1910) commanding, led the advance of the 354th Infantry, with the Second Battalion under Major Victor Whitside in support and the Third Battalion under Major Harvey B. Stivers in reserve.

By the time the Second Battalion was fully deployed and advancing, the enemy artillery either saw us or were informed of our whereabouts. The advance was made across a nearly flat open plain towards Beney. Except for fairly heavy artillery fire there was no opposition from the enemy. The big shells exploding in the heavy black soil threw great geysers of dirt high in the air; actually they looked worse than they were, due to the nature of the ground upon which they were falling. Had it been rocky, our losses would have been very great. We pushed forward for three-quarters of a mile north of Beney to a position selected by General Winn that morning. The 353rd Infantry advanced just beyond to our right, and the 355th extended the line to our left. At these points the advance was stopped for the day and we began to entrench. It was then about 9:00 a.m. The village of Beney being in my regimental sector, I took it as headquarters.

At 7:16 a.m., just as the advance began, I wrote the following message to Major Whitside, "Keep your battalion not less than 1,000 yards in rear of leading battalion. Move it on a front of at least 700 yards." It must be remembered that at this time the 354th Infantry was not well instructed in the new attack formation and I was fearful that the battalions themselves and the regiment as a whole would be crowded with resulting casualties. At 10:55 a.m. the commanding officer of the First Battalion was sent this message. "The right of your line should be 600 yards northwest of Xammes in liaison with 353rd. You have been given a front of about 600 yards running northwest. The center of your line is just about on the crossroad of two country roads 1,000 yards from Xammes. If you are crowded occupy all the ground left between the 353rd and 355th and send the other troops several hundred yards to the rear. Push your outposts as far to the front as possible. If the Second Battalion is too close to you, tell Major Whitside to move it to the rear several hundred yards. Make everybody dig in, rolling kitchens are coming up today. Will send out hot coffee and food as soon as possible. Am coming out in a short time to inspect."

After the advance had stopped I walked along the front line to see if everything was going well. The enemy artillery was still strafing us but not too heavily. Men were digging themselves into foxholes and seemed in high spirits. One young soldier I remember very distinctly. He wasn't digging, he was praying or reading a pocket edition of the New Testament. From somewhere he had gathered a stone about the size of a grapefruit; with his nose almost touching this solid object he lay in the deep grass with his open book before him. I stopped beside him and realized just how he felt. That little solid stone, to him, represented physical protection from the bursting shells. Little did he realize that the stone, against which he held his face, was really the only danger he had to fear (outside of a direct hit) from the enemy's long range artillery fire. I explained to the young man what might happen if a shell burst near him and the blast blew that stone into his face. He threw it away and I left him, both of us trusting in the Almighty. I have often wondered if a kind Providence also spared him.

Later that day while I was in Beney the enemy increased their shelling and the Second Battalion, without orders, left their position and fell back behind the Beney-Thiaucourt road. When I went up to inspect the line in the late afternoon I couldn't find them; found instead some of the 353rd Infantry and then learned of the retreat of Whitside's battalion. It seems that in withdrawing they came upon Colonel Reeves who was somewhere behind his regiment. He stopped them and sent them back to the Beney-Thiaucourt road. Not a word or sign of this did any of us hear or see at regimental headquarters in Beney, and as I have stated only learned of it when endeavoring to find the battalion at the front. The retreat might have had serious consequences, to say the least. The battalion commander was responsible and I started to relieve him, but was persuaded not to do so by the division chief of staff, Colonel Charles E. Kilbourne (1898). Beney is a tiny village, the little house we were occupying at headquarters was on the eastern side of the village, and how the retreat of the Second Battalion occurred without some of us seeing it I cannot understand. Naturally I was not only angry but disillusioned. I never learned just how the withdrawal started, but apparently Major Whitside considered the position too exposed and on his own initiative ordered the withdrawal, which according to Colonel Reeves became very disorderly. Kilbourne said that except for the effect on the morale of the regiment no actual harm had been done, and he urged me to let the matter drop, which I did. Major Whitside died of flu about two months later after the Armistice, in Germany.

I was told by a captain of the 353rd Infantry that the diamond shaped formation had worked fine, and a French observer was reported as having said he had never seen a finer deployment in battle. As soon as conditions warranted I began training the 354th battalions in the same formation. By working with the companies in support and reserve, and these alternated with front line organizations, the entire regiment soon was proficient in the attack formation.

By 11:00 a.m. of the thirteenth the infantry of the Eighty-ninth Division was holding a line of individual foxholes from just north of Xammes to a narrow gauge railroad in the Dampvitoux woods northwest of Xammes. Total length of line was about two miles. Each regiment had approximately a half mile front. The 177th Brigade held the most exposed section of the front, there being little or no cover, and the enemy kept up the artillery fire all during the daylight hours. During the night of September 13–14, our men continued to entrench only to have to repeat the work 1 ¼ miles farther forward on the night of September 14–15. That night the division engineers laid out the trace of a standing trench. We sent working parties forward and by daylight they were partially entrenched.

From then on, digging and stringing wire was the order of the day and night, and in spite of the fact that the American soldier loathes digging, the 354th soon had a very decent line of trenches for both the front and support battalions.

The enemy had retired to what was known as the Hindenburg Line. In our front the Germans were entrenched on the general line Charey—Domartin—Dampvitoux. Between the opposing outpost positions there was a no-man's-land of from 800 to 1,200 yards. Although Beney was not within six or seven miles of the enemy light artillery, the little village received a daily pounding, and fragments from the shells bursting on the hard street or stone walls wounded or killed many men, some of whom had no business in the village. A woman of the Red Cross came into the village and set up a hot chocolate stand. Of course that brought in a crowd of soldiers, and an enemy shell got several of them belonging to the 355th Infantry (on our left) before this kind but perilous enterprise was stopped.

3

On the fourteenth, division headquarters directed me to have a battalion make an after dark reconnaissance in the direction of the Charey-Dommartin line to test its strength, take prisoners, etc. In my opinion this was too large and inexperienced a force to undertake a raid to the enemy's line, probably have a bit of a fight and then withdraw. Moving troops in any form of extended order, after dark, is difficult even in a friendly country. Against an active alert enemy the chance that parts of the force might get lost, fire into other sections or be ambushed by enemy patrols was not unlikely. My request to send a force of not over one company was refused. Major Bridges with the First Battalion then in reserve was selected and I carefully informed him what was wanted, advised him to march on compass bearings, and about the distances between organizations; but I did not warn him about the danger of attempting to deploy or extend the platoons. As Bridges was a Regular Army officer I assumed he knew how necessary it was not to get lost or have the different companies lose touch with one another. I blame myself for not telling him in detail just what force to use in front, where to halt his support. The reconnaissance was a complete failure, no part of it got near the enemy line. Major Bridges deployed the battalion just as he would have done in broad daylight. The platoons marched in artillery columns, got lost and it is remarkable that the wandering detachments did not fire at each other. Fortunately this calamity was escaped.

Shortly after the fiasco reconnaissance of the fifteenth I organized a regimental patrol group under Second Lieutenant Marshall F. Wilder (H Company). It consisted of 60 men, all volunteers, drawn from the entire regiment. Later the strength was increased to 100 men, and First Lieutenant Herman L. McNulty (M Company) was appointed second in command, Wilder having been promoted to captain for his efficient execution of a raid of the twenty-sixth of September. Before the patrol group carried out this special raid they had made nightly expeditions up to and along the enemy lines for over a week, one-third going out each night. The group lived in Bouillonville with the rear echelon of the regimental headquarters, where they could get three hot meals daily. We all might sleep two nights out of three and a day's sleep after the night patrol. Just as the Australians did in the Hamel sector in July, so operated the 354th patrol group. No-man's-land was ours in our sector.

A few days before September 26, I was called down to division headquarters in Euvezin and told by the chief of staff, Colonel John C. H. Lee (W.P. 1909), that General Wright wished me to arrange a night raid on the division front. That the raiding party was to penetrate the enemy line. To give the enemy an impression that the entire division was attacking, division headquarters arranged for a heavy fire of artillery on the entire front of the division, to fall on the enemy front line at 11:30 p.m., September 25. This barrage conformed to others from all the American divisions in line from the Argonne to Verdun to our front to the Vosges. After six hours of steady bombardment, at 5:30 a.m. September 26 the barrage was to roll forward until the commanding officer of the raiding party fired a pre-arranged Very light signal, when the artillery would cease firing and the raiding party withdrew. I was told to select any portion of the front I considered most suitable and to assume entire charge of the maneuver.

After talking the matter over with Wilder, I selected Charey as the raiders' objective. Opposite the right of our line and about 300 yards northeast of it was a bluff, sixty or eighty feet high, which formed the southern end of what was called the plateau of Grande Fontaine. At the top of this bluff the Germans had their outpost line covering the approach to Charey, about 1,100 yards to the northeast. Wilder's patrols had reconnoitered this area several times and were familiar with the terrain between our lines and the enemy. Wilder was directed to move his party after dark on the twenty-fifth and before 11:00 p.m. to this bluff, to remain there all night, and at 5:30 a.m. the next morning to advance up the bluff, attack the German outpost and drive them into Charey. Having accomplished this he was to fire a Very light signal, which would be repeated by the C.O., First Battalion and by regimental headquarters, notifying the artillery to stop firing over the entire division front.

There was a chance that during the night the enemy might discover the presence of this raiding party, which would have put them on the alert and made the early morning attack more difficult, but after 11:00 p.m. when the concentrated fire of many guns was plastering the German lines I had little fear that any German patrols would venture into no-man's-land. The great advantage of starting the attack from less than a 100 yards of the enemy outposts was the fact that any counter barrage their artillery might lay down during the night to break up an infantry attack couldn't possibly fall on our men, and at 5:30 a.m. when the barrage lifted, the Germans would expect the Americans to appear some distance out in no-man's-land and would be at a great disadvantage when the Americans appeared simultaneously with the lifting of the barrage. Looking at this bluff from our front lines gave me the idea of posting the patrol against its steep slope, instead of in our own lines or a short distance in front of them. Our artillery was cautioned about their fire on this bluff section of the German line. Any ballistic error they might make elsewhere was of no interest to us, but on the bluff against which Wilder's 100 men were lying no American shells must fall and none did.

In preparation for the raid division headquarters asked me what assistance it could give, and I asked for some hospital corps men trained in first aid to the wounded. These 15 men were to report at regimental headquarters in Xammes early in the evening of the twenty-fifth; from there they would be taken to a point west of the village where Wilder and his patrol would wait for them. Sometime after the scheduled hour for their arrival in Xammes, Major Meade telephoned from his aid station that the litter bearers had just arrived, and was told to send them over to our P.C. Sitting in my little room I presently heard the rasping sounds of hobnailed shoes on stone and hard sand and was just starting to go out into the street to meet the detachment when a German shell moaned its way over Xammes en route to some place far in rear. Immediately the street was filled with excited voices and the hobnailed shoe sounds indicated rapid flight. It was quite dark but only a few yards from our door I saw a black something on the road and going nearer found it to be a soldier pancaked in the dust and debris of our village highway. Sending men of our headquarters out to search the immediate vicinity we rounded up all but one or two of the original 15 litter bearers. They were badly scared and although entirely unfamiliar with the architecture of Xammes' ruins had managed, in the flight of a shell, to disappear in a highly efficient "hide and seek" manner. Later we learned of their previous war experience, which was nil. They had only very recently landed in France and reported to the division surgeon, had never been under fire or near the front. Suddenly, after dark, they found themselves in a ghost village near the front, the skeletons of stone buildings lined the deadly quiet street then the whine of the big shell, which as far as their knowledge of artillery fire went seemed about to fall on them. Their reaction was natural and although at the time I knew nothing about them I had seen too much of the American soldier under fire not to know at once that these hospital corps men were the greenest of rookies.

Gathering them together I endeavored to explain the methodical German method of strafing, that Xammes was not due for any for another half hour, all they had to do was follow the sergeant who would lead them out of town to the soft earth where Lieutenant Wilder and his patrol were assembled. They listened but not all believed me, for as they turned off the street into the open country to the west another shell flew overhead and again they scattered.

Not knowing what the enemy reaction would be to our six-hour strafing of his area, I took some of the staff to Major Meade's house, sending the rest out of the village. The C.O., First Battalion, was directed to have an officer and a platoon with a machine gun report to Lieutenant Wilder at a designated place at 9:00 p.m. This reinforcement was not to be used in the raid but was posted well out in no-man's-land as a support.

Wilder divided his party into three groups. The left under Sergeant John Bargfrede (H Company), right under Sergeant Roy C. Anthony (B Company), while he commanded the center group as well as the entire raiding party. Long before 1:00 p.m. these groups were lying quietly on the southern slope of the bluff. At 5:30 a.m., with the lifting of the barrage, they dashed up the bluff, surprised the Germans and by 6:00 a.m. had entered the outskirts of Charey. The center and right groups met the strongest resistance, but in spite of the ten machine guns encountered as well as some 60 of the enemy they had the Germans on the run in about ten minutes. Two Germans were captured, about twenty killed. The machine guns being too heavy to carry were disabled by firing rifle shots into the mechanism. About 5:30 a.m. I took a runner and armed with a Very pistol and cartridges went east of the village where there was a clear view of the country in the direction of Charey. I could hear the roar of the big shells passing overhead and see the smoke and dirt their bursts made on the plateau north of the bluff. As I suspected, the enemy very soon began to plaster our front line with artillery, but Wilder wasn't there and only a part of the advance post position command. Most of the garrison I had directed to withdraw temporarily the night before; we lost no one from that shelling. At or about 6:00 a.m. Very light stars burst into view near Charey. To be sure it was Wilder. Because the Germans might happen to fire the same type of stars I waited until it was repeated. Then I fired the signal and shortly afterwards the artillery fire ceased. The front line battalion commander was also supposed to repeat the cease fire signal from the raiders but he apparently couldn't see Wilder's signal as no Very light signal was seen over our front line.

As I walked back to Meade's station, a German scout, or what we would call now a day's fighting plane, buzzed very low over Xammes. Evidently he was endeavoring to ascertain whether the whole division was attacking or preparing to attack. As he roared down the road just above the housetops I flattened myself against a house wall to avoid any machine gun bullets he might feel like sending me at this early hour, but he was in a hurry, didn't fire a shot and the last I saw of him he was accelerating the gas explosions en route for home to report, probably, that the Eighty-ninth Division had been bluffing and that now it was all over. If we and many other divisions had been endeavoring to fool the Germans (and according to later reports, succeeded), the faraway sound of heavy artillery firing showed that up in the Argonne the American divisions were not bluffing.

The raiding party had one man killed and eleven wounded. The man killed was, I believe, one of the hospital corps men. The returning raiders were in fine fettle upon the success of their well executed and courageous stab at the enemy, and we at the regimental P.C. were congratulating ourselves on the little victory and the relatively small loss, when the brigade commander, General Winn, sent me a note directing me to explain why the 354th headquarters was "Wholly out of reach with brigade commander for five hours during the night of September 25–26." That was the recognition we received for what we considered not a badly directed and planned night operation.

Eight

The New Army

1

On October 12, 1918, the Eighty-ninth Division was transferred from the III to the V corps and ordered to march across country to the vicinity of Eclisfontaine and Epinonville about ten miles to the northwest (due west of Montfaucon). Leaving the Recicourt area on the morning of the twelfth we started for the new sector. The distance was nothing; the terrain was terrible. The entire area was an ex-battleground. In fact the American attack of the twenty-sixth of September started on the ground we had to march over. I say "marched over" but actually it was more of a migration. Orders required we move on a broad front with a long distance between organizations (platoons and companies). The country was covered with trenches and barbed wire; our progress was both laborious and slow. We made about five miles the first day, bivouacking near the village of Very. The rolling kitchens and other animal-drawn transportation followed the road towards Varennes, but the traffic was so heavy and so many traffic jams occurred that we saw nothing of them until late the next day. Emergency rations and what food the individual men carried was all we had for some thirty-six hours.

Resuming the trek on the fourteenth, we were bivouacked in the woods in the triangle Gesnes-Epinonville-Eclisfontaine that afternoon.

On the sixteenth General Wright gave a short talk to the officers and noncommissioned officers of the regiment. He rode up in front of the group and told the corporals to move up in front. "Because it is upon you corporals that our success depends." He asked them if they would put it across, and they answered with a powerful "we will."

Later that morning all the Eighty-ninth Division officers were assembled to hear a talk by General Summerall. We assembled near a road, in the mud, and the corps commander drove up in his Cadillac limousine. Feeling more than ever resentful over his treatment of me three months before, I could not help compare his fine car, his warmly clad figure and dry uniform to the wet and mud-coated uniforms of the hundreds of officers who had spent the past six days sleeping in the cold mud of the Argonne and eating under the almost continuous rains of October. He was greeted by General Wright, and then he stepped forward and in his best pontifical manner said, "Good morning, gentlemen. I am glad to see you. I hope to see some of you again not all of you, but some of you." He then went on to tell how he had visited battalions that had failed to take their objectives, but they never had been able to give a good excuse for their failures. "As long as one man stands there is no excuse," he said.

Of course I realized he was talking heroics to men who were about to go into a fierce struggle after just five days of freedom from shell fire since August 6; that these officers and men were spending their days on cold wet ground and sleeping on it under their little tents, eating under the dripping trees or crouched in their "dog tents." I knew, as he did, that there are few if any instances where 100 percent of an attacking force destroys itself in an attack, that 25 to 30 percent is a big loss. I knew, although he didn't, that for an ex-artillery officer to stand forth before fighting infantry soldiers and in a deep resonant voice tell them how to fight, how he expected only "some" of them to survive, and that as long as any one of them could stand he would not accept their failure to capture their objective, was the poorest exhibition of battle leadership possible to make.

It was well known among infantrymen that members of artillery brigades saw few casualties. Typical was the experience of Captain Harry S. Truman of Battery D in the Thirty-fifth Division, who began with two hundred men in his unit and took home 199, with one death caused by illness, not incurred in line of duty.

On our left we were in contact with the right of the Forty-second Division. We held the southwest edge of the Bois de Bantheville, while the 178th Brigade was to our right deep in the woods. This brigade and later the 353rd Infantry had to fight for two or three days before they managed to drive the enemy completely out of their section of the Bois de Bantheville.

We found a huge dugout and except that its front door faced the enemy lines, that deep safe concrete affair was our home for the next ten days. We mounted a captured German light machine gun at the top of the steps leading down to our P.C., and often we had a shot at some low flying enemy scouting plane. The big dugout consisted of two long narrow corridors, each having its ground exit, connected by a third one near the front; here at a long table we did the necessary and unnecessary and everlastingly required paperwork. The dugout held about 48 bunks and large numbers of our headquarters force, besides the commissioned staff, slept in it, and the gas coughs and the snoring were unique and unsurpassed. Army blankets hung at the foot of the concrete steps provided us with some protection against gas, but fortunately of all the gas shells thrown in the area during our ten days of occupancy none fell near enough to the P.C. to let the gas drop down the stairs to add its aroma to the damp, musty, fetid odors of that Argonne forest home.

All through the woods there were little wooden shacks. Our enemy, prior to the American offensive, seemed to have lived most comfortably and some of our men, including our headquarters mess detail, occupied some of these shacks. We ate all our meals at a long table in a nearby shed, running for cover if the enemy was so impolite as to shell us at mealtimes.

In the morning, before breakfast, it was quite a sight to see everyone out under the trees, their little mirrors hanging from branches, shaving. The Second Division, which had been designated to jump off for the coming attack from the area held by the Forty-second Division, sent a young Marine officer over to my headquarters as liaison officer. Evidently shaving in the morning wasn't the custom in his own outfit. For two mornings he watched us, then of his own accord, or possibly at the hint of some young member of my staff, he, too, hung up his little mirror.

The enemy shelled the entire area systematically, often mixing up mustard gas shells with the high explosive. In consequence, the damp brush and tree-covered hollows were constantly sending forth gas fumes. Runners, company food and ammunition carriers, road-building engineer troops, and signal working parties were absorbing more and more gas daily.

By 1918 the Germans were expert at gassing American and Allied troops and a favorite technique was what Babcock describes here, mixing high-explosive shells with mustard gas. Another, which he observed, was exposing them to small gas attacks that slowed their activities and built up a tiredness, more and more fatigue, that could make ineffective the work of entire divisions. The Forty-second Division's first assignment in the Battle of the Meuse-Argonne, October 1–31, saw its 84th Brigade take the Côte (or hill) of Chatillon on October 16, in which it broke through the Kriemhilde Stellung, the middle and best fortified area of the Hindenburg Line. But after the breakthrough the division was so weak from exposure to gas that it could barely hold the territory it had taken in the middle of the month.

Every morning, followed by one of the regimental runners, I inspected some portion of the front or support battalion positions. Knowing that the enemy shelled the area on a schedule, which of course he probably changed frequently, I would try to arrange my arrival in any section at a time when the attention of the German artillery was not due. Several times the runner and I have sat on a log in the forest, smoked cigarettes and heard the shells bursting in the area we intended visiting. When the enemy got that bit of strafing out of his system we continued our walk.

In addition to the rather high angle, long distance shelling, the enemy used an Austrian gun of very high velocity, called by the soldiers a "whiz-bang." This nickname accurately describes that gun and its fast moving shell. To have one of those shells pass nearby was rather terrifying. It whizzed by at high speed, bursting with a tremendous crash. Then, what seemed seconds later, came the dull report of the discharge from the gun.

The "high angle"gun was a howitzer; having a lower muzzle velocity than a gun like the French 75 it delivered curved fire.

As we expected a forward movement very soon, no effort was made to construct regular trenches. Our front line was a series of foxholes or funk-holes for one or more men. In rear of the platoons the platoon commanders had their holes, perhaps covered with brush or a shelter half. The company commanders were centrally located as regards their front line platoons and the platoons used as immediate support for the front line. Still farther to the rear was the battalion P.C., another temporary shelter. Each company sent their runners to their battalion P.C. In this way all the runners learned the most direct route to their battalion commander. One or two of these runners remained at the battalion P.C. while the remainder returned to their company. The platoon commanders followed the same routine between themselves and their company commander. Regimental headquarters sent runners to the front line and support battalion commanders, and in addition our P.C. was in telephone connection with the P.C. of each battalion and by telephone, wireless and runners with the P.C. of the brigade.

The rear echelon of headquarters and the supply company was in Gesnes. The supply company was commanded at this time by Captain Raymond E. LaDriere, a most efficient and energetic officer and a great supply rustler. We were absolutely dependent on the supply company for food, ammunition, grenades, picks and shovels, flares, sandbags.

On the twenty-first my regiment extended its front to the left, taking over the ground held by the 165th Infantry of the Forty-second Division.

Enemy shelling was fairly constant and widely scattered over the area. The trees had lost most of their leaves and enemy planes had little difficulty locating our lines in the too densely populated woods and spotting for the artillery, and we had severe casualties almost daily.

I endeavored to get authority from the brigade to echelon our forces in much greater depth, just to hold the front line with a few outposts and withdraw the front line battalion to the position of the support battalion, and to move the latter well in rear of the Romagne-Sommerance road. This recommendation was only partially granted, as I now remember. I was authorized to move the support troops south of the Romagne-Sommerance road, but the front line battalion (Second) continued to have many casualties. On the night of the twenty-fourth-twenty-fifth it suffered heavy gas casualties.

Bantheville constituted a salient into the German line and because of the special carrying parties with the heavy marmite cans of coffee and food it was possible to argue that the Eighty-ninth, waiting to move forward, was paying more for this territory than it was worth. The plan for attack was for the Second to replace the Forty-second at the last moment. As matters turned out, the Eighty-ninth gained no advantage by being, as was the case, higher than the Second because of its Bantheville salient, as once the Second broke through the German line it moved up rapidly and came abreast in a day or so–marked by lack of liaison on the Second's part, creating worry in its sister V Corps division. The Eighty-ninth could not retreat because of the policy of First Army, insisted upon by General Pershing, of no retreat from ground once taken. Babcock's suggestion of thinning out his front line was probably too close to this ban.

One cold wet night about 8:00 p.m., a message was received from the brigade directing me to submit a map of our area showing the location of the P.C.'s of all front line units, including the posts of command of the lieutenants or sergeants commanding platoons. It is things like that that harass an officer in wartime. As I have previously described, each platoon commander had a hole in the ground near the other holes occupied by the men of his platoon. He knew where all his men were. The company commander knew where the four platoon commanders were, the battalion commander knew where his four company commanders were, and I knew where the three battalion commanders were. As a matter of fact I also knew where many other subordinate commanders were located, as I had visited them frequently. However all I really needed to know officially was the exact location of the battalion P.C.'s and all the brigade needed to know or should have cared about knowing was where Colonel Reeves and myself were located. But occasionally General Winn (who by late October became a major general) would forget his rank and position and bother the life out of his two colonels with matters of no possible concern to him and his staff.

Ordinarily when a brigade commander was promoted he left the division for duties commensurate with his new rank. To the relief

of General Wright, Winn promised to stay with his brigade until the forthcoming action, the last attack in the Battle of the Meuse-Argonne, as it turned out, was over. Wright's concern for Winn's presence was in part his increasing dissatisfaction with his other brigade commander, Hanson, whom eventually he relieved.

I read the order, probably muttered a damn or two, and then told the staff officers present that what I intended doing was not to be taken as a strictly correct compliance with orders, but in view of the time of night, weather, etc., I would make the map myself, from memory. In ten minutes I marked the approximate positions of 16 platoons, 4 company and 1 battalion P.C.'s, called up a runner and sent General Winn the information that was of absolutely no use to him. If any of his staff wondered how we got the dope so fast, they never inquired.

Having been sent into the line to attack the strong enemy position west and south of the Meuse River, we at regimental headquarters spent many hours daily reconnoitering the "jump-off" front line position. I decided that the assault troops should assemble in front of our foxhole front line in the open land extending for some 1,000 yards to the Landres-et-St. Georges-La Dhuy Farm road. The enemy had machine gun nests scattered through this area, but I believed the front line attacking troops would be safer there, while waiting for "H" hour, than back in the woods should the enemy guess our intentions and put down a heavy counter barrage. Shell fragments are bad enough, but the mixture of steel and flying tree trunks and branches is worse.

The nearest German machine gun nest to our lines in this open country was, as I remember, about 300 yards distant. To drive these guns farther back I arranged with the division to have a 6-inch gun battery put down a strafing fire on their positions. Well before the hour when this was to be done, Barnard and I walked up into the Bantheville woods and selected a position in our front line on the edge of the woods where we had a clear view of the ground to be cannonaded.

At the hour set for the strafing, the first shells came over and fell in the territory occupied by the enemy, bursting and throwing up tall columns of black dirt. The next salvo or group fell nearer our own lines, and then to my horror and disgust, each succeeding shell burst closer and closer to the edge of the woods until finally the shells were falling squarely on our own front line.

Of course, the moment I saw the shells falling short I sent my runner on the run, back to the telephone of the front line battalion commander to notify the artillery what they were doing. The telephone was about a mile away, as we were on the flank of the line while the battalion P.C. was centrally located. I do not remember how many rounds of high explosive our artillery intended firing, but long before the runner could have reached the telephone the shelling stopped. The front line platoon commanders in the area withdrew their men as the shells began to fall short, so there were no casualties.

I went back to the division and made a strong complaint about the inefficiency of the artillery. They countered by blaming their inaccuracies on the deterioration of the powder behind the 6-inch shells. It is hard to refute such excuses, but a careful organization, not having full confidence in the powder, would have had an artillery observer with a telephone in the front line and at the first indication of short shooting he would have telephoned for an increase in the range; but to shoot their own infantry out of the trenches did not seem to worry this artillery outfit at all. Artillery that has spent years shooting behind cover, never seeing what they are endeavoring to hit or where their shells are falling, seem to become quite indifferent to ballistic shortcomings—the whole process of loading, setting the sight, firing is mechanical with little or no realization of the fact that they are at war.

The Germans had Prussian Guard divisions in the American sector, and were holding on to their positions for all they were worth. Enemy planes flew over us at all hours and often our airplanes were up at the same time but we never saw them fight each other. Our aviators let the German observation balloons stay up all day. It made the foot soldiers furious to see our planes flying about, burning gasoline and doing nothing; that is, nothing that helped the soldier in the trenches or foxholes. On the afternoon of the twenty-third from a hill near our dugout I watched the attack of a brigade of the Ninetieth Division on our right. The enemy observation balloons were up and saw every move of our soldiers. The air was full of our airplanes but not one made an attempt to put a single balloon down. I have no idea why, except at that time the air service was much taken with the "star" or "ace" business, aviators who had downed several enemy planes, single-handed. When one remembers that there were many thousands of pilots and few "aces", it showed how little real fighting the average pilot took part in the last war. As for keeping the balloons down, it was too dangerous, some of our pilots told me. In 1918 there was little or no cooperation between the ground forces and those in the air in the American Army. In fact, I know of no case where bombing or machine gunning by aviators was attempted in connection with a ground assault. How different it is today.

2

Promptly at 3:30 a.m. on November 1, 1918, the guns opened fire. Some 60,000 shells were fired by the light artillery; in addition the heavy (large caliber) artillery plastered the enemy back areas, while the machine gun companies of the division poured bullets by the hundreds of thousands over our heads and the trees with high angle fire.

I have no adjectives to describe this man-made flying death, the appalling noises of the shells as they swept over us in one continuous flight. In some respects the machine gun bullets were, to us, the most terrifying. My recollection is that the machine guns fired from 3:30 a.m. to 6:30 a.m., then those assigned to the attacking battalions caught up with their organizations and went forward as previously described. The machine gun barrage was terrific. The bullets, following one another in thousands of files, sounded to me like giant shears cutting a mile wide sheet of tin. Although these bullets were clearing the trees under which we waited "H" hour, it really took quite a bit of mental effort to stand up; it was hard to believe those bullets weren't flying right past one's head.

For two hours we sat or lay down under this torrent of lead, steel and high explosive; then, at 5:30 a.m., on the minute, the infantry whistles blew and the assault battalion went forward behind the rolling barrage of our share of the 128 light artillery guns used in the Eighty-ninth Division area. Ten minutes later our first prisoners were met being escorted to the rear. They had been part of the machine gun crews that had annoyed us in the territory between our lines and La Dhuy Farm.

While the First Battalion was in bivouac behind the tree-covered hill north of Gesnes waiting to go forward to the assault position, Captain

Jones and Lieutenant Talbot rode back to a Y.M.C.A. hut in the hope that they could get some supplies for the men, who were lying day-in and day-out in the thick mud. They filled their saddle bags with everything they could carry. It was all paid for in cash, so Jones reported, the "Y" would not even give them a newspaper. The Y was short of cigarettes, but they purchased all the cigars in the hut. These cigars were given to the assault platoons as the two front companies C and D went over the top; almost every man had a cigar clinched between his teeth. Jones said, "This casual touch did much to quiet my own nerves, and perhaps the nerves of others."

The Salvation Army gave away doughnuts; the Y with much more in stock could not do so. The Y received criticism, so much so that after the war it engaged the writer Katherine Mayo to come to its defense. She titled her book *"That Damn Y": A Record of Service* (1920).

For a time I followed the rear of the First Battalion, directing the majority of the advanced echelon to follow the support battalion. Our men were following the heavy barrage closely, and as the curtain lifted and moved forward they moved right in on the shattered enemy. Enemy shelling was not heavy but some shells were bursting in most directions. Before the sun was high there was a mist and a low ceiling. Compasses had been issued all platoon commanders and great stress had been laid on the necessity of carefully following the compass course as prescribed in the attack order. Out in an open field somewhere north of La Dhuy Farm, I saw the support battalion advancing in perfect order, the combat groups marching in single files with intervals and distances well kept, but to me they seemed to be taking a direction many degrees to the right of the one prescribed. Hastening over to the extreme right flank platoon, I said to the young lieutenant, "It seems to me you are way off your course." He glanced down at the compass in his hand and replied, "Right on the course, sir," repeating the bearing. "My mistake," I said, "You are correct; it is I who am lost."

I was carrying over my left arm my raincoat, which was folded several times, and to this is due my escape from what might have been a severe wound. I saw the burst of a shell about 75 yards from me and an instant later something hit me on the left forearm with sufficient force to cut a ragged hole through all the raincoat folds, the sleeve of my blouse, and my flannel shirt, only the long sleeve of my winter underwear went uncut. At my feet I picked up a jagged chunk of steel that must have weighed half a pound. It gave me a sore and black and blue arm, but I was so thankful it hadn't selected a more vital spot than the arm and raincoat.

The Second Division was on our left, having taken over the front of the Forty-second Division during the night of October 31-November 1. As the Eighty-ninth Division jump-off position was considerably in advance of the Second Division, we were given an intermediate objective where the assault battalions of the Eighty-ninth Division were to wait for the Second Division to come up abreast of them and enter the Bois des Hazois. This intermediate objective for the 177th Brigade ran from just south of the Bois d'Andevanne to a point about halfway between La Dhuy Farm and the Hazois wood. It was to be reached at 6:18 a.m. and departed from at 6:30 a.m.

The first objective for our brigade was a line beginning at the north and at the Bois d'Andevanne at Hill 300 and running southwest along the northern edge of a line of small scattered woods to and including the Bergerie Farm, a two kilometer advance. The First Battalion was scheduled to be on this line at 8:00 a.m. and depart there at 8:30 a.m. During the half-hour wait, after capturing the objective, the support companies (A and B) "leap-frogged" the two front companies (C and D) for the assault on the second objective.

The second objective was 2½ kilometers farther north, called the heights of Barricourt (about the center of those dense woods). It was scheduled for capture at 10:55 a.m. Here the support battalion was to leap-frog the First Battalion and move forward at 12:20 p.m., a delay of one hour and twenty-five minutes. This was done to allow for failure to capture an objective on schedule, and by holding the barrage on the second objective the chances were that it would not get away from the following troops before they were ready to advance.

The third and last objective for November 1 was a line from Les Tuilleries Farm on the Andevanne-Tailly road along the northern edge of the Bois de Barricourt to some high ground called La Polarde about 1,000 yards south of the village of Barricourt. At 7:25 a.m. Captain Jones reported by runner, "Waiting for barrage to take first objective." That meant he was waiting for the barrage to move on, so his command could capture the position without doing so under the fire of their own artillery. At 8:10 a.m. when my marching P.C. was on the Bantheville-Remonville road about two kilometers from the latter village Jones reported by runner, "Reached first objective at 8:00 a.m. few casualties. Companies reforming and will move on when barrage advances at 8:30 a.m. P.C. now at 04.8–90.I. Prisoners from 246th and 352nd Infantry." At 9:00 a.m., by runner, a message was sent to the commanding officer of the support battalion reminding him that the First Battalion was due to capture the second objective at 10:55 a.m. It was on this objective that the Third Battalion was to leap-frog the First Battalion and at 12:20 p.m. take up the advance. I cautioned the Third Battalion commander not to crowd the assault battalion, to keep at least 1,000 yards behind them. He was also informed that I thought the men were doing splendidly.

At 9:10 a.m. Jones reported "We are advancing and taking our objectives as per schedule. Troops are now crossing ravine southeast of Remonville." This was the area of very heavy fighting.

The Third Battalion was now under the command of one of the young company commanders, Captain Hugh M. Pinkerton. To suddenly be given command of a big battalion in action was a great responsibility. I realized his difficulties and at 9:10 a.m. sent him this message: "Remember your barrage starts for the third objective at 12:20 p.m. Be sure to keep great width and great depth. In the woods follow the barrage closely with patrols. Try to gain north edge of Bois de Barricourt by passing around west edge of woods with a company. Mop it up later."

The Third Battalion went forward and after a bitter struggle in the dense forest of Barricourt, where the enemy had deep trenches and dugouts and snipers fought from trees, drove them out of the Bois de Barricourt in our front and down the slopes to the north towards the villages of Barricourt and Tailly. We were on our third objective. It was beginning to get dark, the wet November fog enveloped us and it was apparent that the fighting was over for the time being.

Our long-range guns had blown huge craters in the wet heavy soil of the area, and in these natural defense positions the Third Battalion settled down for the night. The left of our line rested near the hill, "La Polarde," just south of Barricourt. Captain Wilder's company (H) of the Second Battalion was there. This company had been designated as the liaison group, between the right of the Second Division and the left of the Eighty-ninth Division. I went up to the top of this hill to find out what was holding us up in that vicinity and what had become of the Second Division. I noticed three of our soldiers kneeling behind one another in file, just over the top of the hill. I asked Wilder why they remained so exposed to enemy fire, and his answer was that they were all dead, all killed in an attempt to take a machine gun nest just beyond the little hill. The instantaneous death of three men, still kneeling close together: by peeking just over the top of the hill I wasn't ten feet from them. The men and their positions were so life-like it was difficult to believe they were not waiting for an opportunity to rise and run forward.

Back in the north edge of Remonville, where the telephone to brigade and division had been brought, the regimental P.C. was established for the night. The only food anyone in the battalions or at our P.C. had was what the individual carried. Personally I have no recollection of eating anything except an apple or some fruit I found in Remonville as we entered it before noon; but all of us carried some food and the emergency ration was also carried by many. Under the stress and responsibility of directing the attack of a big regiment in an all day battle, the lack of food was the least of one's troubles. But could it have been obtained, hot coffee and hot army "slum" meat and vegetables would have built up strength and stamina in our weary officers and men.

At 7:40 p.m. General Winn sent the following message to his brigade, "General Wright wishes to express to the command his hearty congratulations and thanks."

About 8:00 p.m. orders went out to Captain Pinkerton that the Second Battalion would make the assault the next morning. That the barrage would fall 500 meters beyond the line marked on the map as the third objective at 5:30 a.m., remain stationary until 5:40 a.m. and then move forward.

I was doubtful that the Third Battalion was accurately on the third objective but it was on the line for all practical purposes. Where the open country, which sloped north, was cut up into little ravines, the Third Battalion was holding the high ground in combat groups occupying shell holes. The First Battalion had been withdrawn to the vicinity of Remonville and Second Battalion was in the woods behind the Third Battalion.

During the night the commanding officer of the Third Battalion was ordered to push strong patrols to his front to keep contact with the enemy and get prisoners; this was the brigade order.

Captain Pinkerton was also notified that his battalion with Company A of the 341st Machine Gun Battalion (the 177th Brigade M.G. Battalion) would act as support for the Second Battalion, which he was to follow at 1,200 yards, that at 4:00 a.m. on the second he was to have four guides at his P.C. to get the Second Battalion companies forward to their attack positions. The regimental machine gun company was attached to the Second Battalion for the assault. I had Captain Root and Lieutenant Fickett of the M.G. company and Lieutenant Fletcher, commanding the 37-mm. guns, report to me in Remonville, and the assault order for the morning was gone over with them, and Lieutenant Colonel Barnard was directed to see that Captain Root and his battalion started promptly with the barrage as it moved forward at 5:40 a.m.

At 5:30 a.m. November 2, I heard a few artillery shells from our side passing overhead and I knew that was the beginning of the morning assault. Captain Wolff and I started immediately for the front via the dirt road leading to Barricourt. At the north edge of the woods Colonel Barnard met me and said that as no barrage had been laid down by our artillery the Second Battalion had made no effort to go forward.

That was a fine state of affairs, and I blamed myself for not being on hand at 5:30 a.m. It was then after six o'clock and the little, ineffective barrage had rolled itself forward and only the sounds of the few shells being sent over indicated that our artillery was still firing.

The Third Battalion still held the ground captured the afternoon of November 1, the Second Battalion was in the Barricourt woods. Wolff and I found Captain Pinkerton in a shell hole 400 yards north of the edge of the woods and just east of the Remonville-Barricourt road. Captain Root was sent for, and I sent a runner to our right with a message addressed to "Any officer of the 353rd Infantry," asking the reader to let me know, by our runner, the answer to the question, "Where is your front line?" Sometime later we learned that the 353rd assault battalion had not advanced.

As soon as Root had scrambled down into this huge shell hole I ordered him to prepare to move forward immediately. General Winn with one or two staff officers appeared about this time and he, too, slid down in the now pretty well crowded shell hole. After hearing what had happened he directed that no advance be attempted until he could get artillery support. We talked the situation over, but neither of us knew what was going on to the left (west) of us where the Second Division was supposed to be. In fact the liaison within the 177th Brigade and with the Second Division had ceased to function.

While we were talking the enemy artillery was throwing shells in our direction. At first this did not appear to be aimed at our huge shell hole, but it wasn't long before the falling shells indicated that the enemy gunners were correcting their range on us by the well known bracketing system. This shell hole was, in the center, about six feet deep with a diameter of perhaps twelve feet, and had been made, probably, by one of our big 8-inch guns or mortars. There must have been at least a dozen officers lining its sloping bank. The burst of a 77-mm. shell in our midst would have made quite a mess. Finally, when one of the ranging shots hit almost on the lip of the hole, sending a shower of dirt over us, I persuaded General Winn to leave. As soon as he disappeared over the edge I got up and climbed up the bank and started for the woods south of us. Before I had taken a dozen steps the enemy fired their battery salvo. The four shells just cleared the big hole, and not one of them missed me by twenty feet. Fortunately the ground was wet, heavy and free of stones; those four shells burst simultaneously, showered me with dirt, scared me almost to death, but I was unhurt. Before another salvo could arrive, all but Pinkerton and his staff had evacuated his P.C., and the enemy observers seeing the running figures of men probably decided the hole was empty; they ceased firing on it.

It is difficult to recall in much detail or sequence the events of this day. It took ages to get any artillery fire on the many machine gun nests in our front. Our 37-mm. guns and Stokes mortars came up and did some effective firing from time to time. I have copies of two of the orders issued in an attempt to gain ground. The first written at 11:45 a.m. to Captain Root said, "Organize at once three or four combat patrols under vigorous leaders. Push them forward at once firing. Try your right flank. We must go forward it is absolutely necessary to get your command forward pass by the nests." Little was accomplished; however, a short advance was made but tired men unaccustomed to attacking without heavy artillery support were not up to it. Later Captain Pinkerton was ordered to organize three large strong combat groups and to pass them east of the woods north of the Tuilleries Farm. This was in the 353rd area, but it was believed that these patrols could work around to their left and get behind the guns holding us up. This, too, brought no known results. In fact we made little progress all of that long hectic day.

We saw nothing of the Second Division, where it was I have no idea, and the history of that famous division throws no light on the subject. The Eighty-ninth Division history states, "It would have been practicable to flank the German position from the left. But this movement would have taken the troops into the sector of the Second Division which it was at the time supposed would shortly be advancing over the ground. The Second Division did not advance during the day, but failure of liaison with that division had prevented word of its plans from reaching the brigade."

After dark I ordered Captain Jones to send a strong platoon to the west of Tailly. This mission was accomplished by Second Lieutenant William E. Maloney of B Company. The enemy apparently began to withdraw after dark on the second, and Lieutenant Maloney's command was able to move into the village of Nouart and was in the village when the advance troops of the 178th Brigade arrived that night. For this and other distinguished services I recommended Maloney for a first lieutanacy.

In May, 1919, when the 354th Infantry started for home, I remained in Europe. Major General Winn, commanding the home-going division, wrote me a very complimentary letter of farewell. I quote one paragraph which bears on the subject of November 2, 1918. "In the Meuse-Argonne offensive, November 1–2, 1918, you led your regiment forward with courage and skill throughout the most violent fighting. On November 2, 1918, you posted yourself with your foremost battalion, in an area swept by shell, machine gun and rifle fire, and personally directed the advance." That was a fine but, I fear, an undeserved compliment about the advance on the second. There was none to brag about and courageous General Winn was there and saw why.

During the night of November 2–3 the 178th Brigade passed through our lines and marched forward, and the 177th Brigade became the reserve. The enemy was in full retreat, seeking to cross the Meuse River; and from now until the eleventh of November we moved northward from village to village as the 178th Brigade made progress before us. The headquarters wagon managed to overtake us on the third, and that evening in our own P.C. in Barricourt, I had General Wright for dinner. He spoke to all of us and was highly pleased with our work.

The regimental losses were very much less than at Soissons in July but nevertheless were heavy. On the fourth I reported to the brigade that my regiment had 91 killed, 271 wounded and 82 missing. Of these latter many were probably killed but had not yet been found. The regiment captured 8 pieces of artillery of 77-mm. caliber, 135 machine guns, 15 Minenwerfers, 318 rifles, 3 auto trucks, 1 auto aircraft gun, large quantities of rifle and machine gun ammunition and grenades, also 653 prisoners.

This prosaic conclusion to Babcock's memoirs fails to catch the triumph of the moment. In which the U.S. Army in 1918, with such leaders as Babcock, with Summerall contributing only blather, took those fine regiments of Americans to victory over the best army in Europe much as Babcock's father sailed from New York in 1856 aboard the clipper ship *Young America*. After three failed attacks in the great Battle of the Meuse-Argonne, as the troops found their way out of the stupidities of the Old Army into the efficiencies of the New, in a fourth and last attack on November 1, with such regiments as Babcock's 354th, they broke the German line and ended the war.

Suggested Further Reading about World War I

Allen, Hervey. *Toward the Flame: A War Diary*. New York: Farrar and Rinehart, 1934.

American Armies and Battlefields in Europe. Washington, D.C.: Government Printing Office, 1938.

Armstrong, David A. *Bullets and Bureaucrats: The Machine Gun and the United States Army, 1861–1916*. Westport, Conn.: Greenwood, 1982.

Asprey, Robert B. *At Belleau Wood*. New York: Harper, 1949.

Ayres, Leonard P., ed. *The War with Germany: A Statistical Summary*. 2nd ed. Washington, D.C.: Government Printing Office, 1919.

Beaver, Daniel R. *Modernizing the American War Department: Changes and Continuity in a Turbulent Era, 1885–1920*. Kent, Ohio: Kent State University Press, 2006.

———. *Newton D. Baker and the American War Effort: 1917–1918*. Lincoln: University of Nebraska Press, 1968.

Braim, Paul F. *The Test of Battle: The American Expeditionary Forces in the Meuse-Argonne Campaign*. Newark: University of Delaware Press, 1987.

Buck, Beaumont B. *Memories of Peace and War*. San Antonio, Tex.: Naylor, 1935.

Bullard, Robert Lee. *Personalities and Reminiscences of the War*. Garden City, N.Y.: Doubleday, Page, 1925.

Chambers, John Whiteclay. *To Raise an Army: The Draft Comes to Modern America*. New York: Free Press, 1987.

Chastaine, Ben H. *History of the 18th U.S. Infantry, First Division: 1812–1919*. New York: Hymans, n.d.

Chinn, George M. *The Machine Gun: History, Evolution, and Development of Manual, Automatic, and Airborne Repeating Weapons*. Washington, D.C.: Government Printing Office, 1951.

Clifford, John Garry. *The Citizen Soldiers: The Plattsburg Training Camp Movement: 1913–1920*. Lexington: University Press of Kentucky, 1972.

Cochrane, Rexmond C. *The 1st Division in the Meuse-Argonne: 1–12 October 1918*. Washington, D.C.: U.S. Army Chemical Corps, 1957.

———. *The 89th Division in the Bois de Bantheville: October 1918*. Washington, D.C.: U.S. Army Chemical Corps, 1960.

———. *The Use of Gas in the Meuse-Argonne Campaign: September-November 1918*.

Washington, D.C.: U.S. Army Chemical Corps, 1958.

Coffman, Edward M. *The Hilt of the Sword: The Career of Peyton C. March*. Madison: University of Wisconsin Press, 1966.

———. *The Old Army: A Portrait of the American Army in Peacetime, 1784–1898*. New York: Oxford University Press, 1986.

———. *The Regulars: The Army Officer, 1898–1941*. Cambridge, Mass.: Harvard University Press, 2004.

———. *The War to End All Wars: The American Military Experience in World War I*. New York: Oxford University Press, 1968.

Cooke, James J. *Pershing and His Generals: Command and Staff in the AEF*. Westport, Conn.: Praeger, 1997.

Cramer, C. H. *Newton D. Baker: A Biography*. Cleveland: World, 1961.

DeWeerd, Harvey A. *President Wilson Fights His War: World War I and the American Intervention*. New York: Macmillan, 1968.

Eisenhower, John S. D. *Yanks: The Epic Story of the American Army in World War I*. New York: Free Press, 2001.

Ferrell, Robert H. *America's Deadliest Battle: Meuse-Argonne 1918*. Lawrence: University Press of Kansas, 2007.

———. *Collapse at Meuse-Argonne: The Failure of the Missouri-Kansas Division*. Columbia: University of Missouri Press, 2004.

———. *Woodrow Wilson and World War I: 1917–1921*. New York: Harper and Row, 1985.

Ferrell, Robert H., ed. *In the Company of Generals: The World War I Diary of Pierpont L. Stackpole*. Columbia: University of Missouri Press, 2009.

Final Report of John J. Pershing: Commander-in-Chief American Expeditionary Forces. Washington, D.C.: Government Printing Office, 1920.

Fleming, Thomas J. *The Illusion of Victory: America in World War I.* New York: Basic Books, 2003.

Grotelueschen, Mark E. *The AEF Way of War: The American Army and Combat in World War I.* New York: Cambridge University Press, 2007.

———. *Doctrine under Trial: American Artillery Employment in World War I.* Westport, Conn.: Greenwood, 2001.

Haber, L. F. *The Poisonous Cloud: Chemical Warfare in the First World War.* Oxford: Clarendon, 1986.

Hamburger, Kenneth E. *Learning Lessons in the American Expeditionary Forces.* Washington, D.C.: U.S. Army Center of Military History, n.d.

Harbord, James G. *The American Army in France: 1917–1919.* Boston: Little, Brown, 1936.

Hawley, Ellis W. *The Great War and the Search for a Modern Order: A History of the American People and Their Institutions, 1917–1933.* New York: St. Martin's, 1979.

Herwig, Holger H. *The First World War: Germany and Austria-Hungary, 1914–1918.* London: Arnold, 1997.

History of the First Division during the World War: 1917–1919. Philadelphia: Winston, 1922.

Johnson, Douglas V., II. "Leadership Prerequisites: Colonel Conrad S. Babcock and Command Development during World War I." In Edward G. Longacre and Theodor J. Zeman, eds. *Beyond Combat: Essays in Military History in Honor of Russell F. Weigley.* Philadelphia: American Philosophical Society, 2007, 104–24.

Johnson, Douglas V., II., and Rolfe E. Hillman Jr. *Soissons: 1918.* College Station: Texas A&M University Press, 1999.

Keegan, John. *The First World War.* New York: Knopf, 1999.

Langer, William L. *Gas and Flame in World War I.* New York: Knopf, 1965.

Lebow, Eileen F. *A Grandstand Seat: The American Balloon Service in World War I.* Westport, Conn.: Praeger, 1998.

Liggett, Hunter. *A.E.F.: Ten Years Ago in France.* New York: Dodd, Mead, 1928.

———. Commanding an American Army: Recollections of the World War. Boston: Houghton Mifflin, 1926.

Marshall, George C. *Memoirs of My Service in the World War: 1917–1918.* James L. Collins Jr., ed. Boston: Houghton Mifflin, 1976.

McGlachlin, Edward E. "Army Artillery in Meuse-Argonne." *Infantry Journal* 23 (1923): 544–52.

Millett, Allan R. *The General: Robert L. Bullard and Generalship in the United States Army, 1881–1925.*

Millett, Allan R., and Williamson Murray, eds. *Military Effectiveness: The First World War.* Boston: Allen & Unwin, 1988.

Neiberg, Michael R. *The Second Battle of the Marne.* Bloomington: Indiana University Press, 2008.

Nenninger, Timothy K. "John J. Pershing and Relief for Cause in the American Expeditionary Forces, 1917–1918." *Army History* (2005): 21–32.

———. "Tactical Dysfunction in the AEF: 1917–1918." *Military Affairs* 51 (1987): 177–81.

———. "Unsystematic as a Mode of Command: Commanders and the Process of Command in the American Expeditionary Forces, 1917–1918." *Journal of Military History* 64 (2000): 739–68.

Palmer, Frederick. *Our Gallant Madness.* Garden City, N.Y.: Doubleday, Doran, 1937.

Pershing, John J. *My Experiences in the World War.* 2 vols. New York: Stokes, 1931.

Pitt, Barrie. *1918: The Last Act.* London: Cassell, 1962.

Rainey, James W. "Ambivalent Warfare: The Tactical Doctrine of the AEF in World War I." *Parameters* 13 (1983): 34–45.

———. "The Questionable Training of the AEF in World War I." *Parameters* 22 (1992–1993): 89–103.

Report of the Secretary of War to the President: 1926. Washington, D.C.: Government Printing Office, 1926.

Scott, E. D. "Gunner in Luzon." *Field Artillery Journal* 29 (Nov.-Dec., 1939): 513–24.

Smith, Gene. *Still Quiet on the Western Front: Fifty Years Later.* New York: Morrow, 1965.

Smythe, Donald. "A.E.F. Snafu at Sedan." *Prologue* 5 (1973): 135–49.

———. *Guerrilla Warrior: The Early Life of John J. Pershing.* New York: Scribner, 1973.

———. *Pershing: General of the Armies.* Bloomington: Indiana University Press, 1988.

Summary of Operations in the World War (by divisions, separately published). Washington, D.C.: Government Printing Office, 1943–1944.

Trask, David F. *The AEF and Coalition Warmaking: 1917–1918*. Lawrence: University Press of Kansas, 1993.

Travers, Tim. *How the War Was Won: Command and Technology in the British Army on the Western Front, 1917–1918*. London: Routledge, 1992.

———. *The Killing Ground: The British Army, the Western Front and the Emergence of Modern Warfare, 1900–1918*. London: Allen & Unwin, 1987.

United States Army in the World War. 17 vols. Washington, D.C.: Government Printing Office, 1948.

Upton, L. S., and Millard E. Tydings. "Capture of Etrayes Ridge: A Machine Gun Study." *Infantry Journal* 31 (1927): 133–36.

Vandiver, Frank E. *Black Jack: The Life and Times of John J. Pershing.* 2 vols. Fort Worth: Texas Christian University Press, 1977.

Van Every, Dale. *The A.E.F. in Battle*. New York: Appleton, 1928.

Venzon, Anne Cipriano, ed. *The United States in the First World War: An Encyclopedia*. New York: Garland, 1995.

Votaw, John F. *The American Expeditionary Forces in World War I.* Oxford: Osprey, 2005.

Weigley, Russell F. *The American Way of War: A History of United States Military Strategy and Policy*. New York: Macmillan, 1973.

———. *History of the United States Army*. New York: Macmillan, 1967.

Wheeler, James Scott. *The Big Red One: The Legendary First Division, from World War I to Desert Storm*. Lawrence: University Press of Kansas, 2007.

Wilson, Dale E. *Treat 'Em Rough: The Birth of American Armor, 1917–20*. Novato, Calif.: Presidio, 1989.

Wright, William M. *Meuse-Argonne Diary: A Division Commander in World War I*. Robert H. Ferrell, ed. Columbia: University of Missouri Press, 2004.

Yockelson, Mitchell A. *Borrowed Soldiers: Americans under British Command, 1918*. Norman: University of Oklahoma Press, 2007.

Zabecki, David T. *Steel Wind: Colonel Georg Bruchmueller and the Birth of Modern Artillery*. Westport, Conn.: Praeger, 1994.

Index